SKETCHING YOUTH, SELF, AND YOUTH WORK

Sketching Youth, Self, and Youth Work

By

Mark Krueger
Youth Work Learning Center,
University of Wisconsin-Milwaukee, USA

SENSE PUBLISHERS
ROTTERDAM / TAIPEI

A C.I.P. record for this book is available from the Library of Congress.

ISBN 978-90-8790-065-6 (paperback)
ISBN 978-90-8790-066-3 (hardback)

Published by: Sense Publishers,
P.O. Box 21858, 3001 AW Rotterdam, The Netherlands
http://www.sensepublishers.com

Printed on acid-free paper

There are things
We live among and to see them
Is to know ourselves

The opening of George Oppen's (2003) poem, *Of Being Numerous,* p. 83

TABLE OF CONTENTS

PREFACE

When I was a child what I saw of the world beyond my immediate neighborhood I saw from the backseat of my parents' car. It was a world glimpsed in passing. It was still. It had its own life and did not know or care that I happened by at that particular time. Like the world of Edward Hopper paintings, it did not return my gaze...These two imperatives—the one that urges us to continue and the one that compels us to stay—create a tension that is constant in Hopper's work (Strand, 2001, p 3).

There are many more influences from literature, philosophy, art, qualitative inquiry, experimental autobiography, youth work, and film that helped me develop the method of reflexivity in this book, but none more important than former US Poet Laureate Mark Strand's (2001) passages about Hopper's paintings, which I had always admired and had been drawn to but didn't quite know why.

INTRODUCTION

I drive by grounds of the residential treatment center where I used to work. The building has been torn down, but the hill on which it stood is still there. We did many things on that hill, the troubled teenage boys and I. We raked leaves, sat, and sledded and rolled down it.

I remember a time when six boys and I had just come back from a park a few blocks away. Things were going well. We were walking up the hill. Below the hill on the other side was the ball diamond and beyond that a small woods and the railroad tracks where the boys tried to run away. Daniel had run there once. I caught him before he could jump a train. He was angry. We had been playing one-on-one basketball and he got upset because I was winning. I "talked him down," and brought him back.

On that day, however, when we approached the center, none of the boys seemed to want to run away. We had had a good time at the park and were hungry. Food I believe was on our minds, the smell of fall leaves in the air. We were moving together in harmony yet separately. Not much was being said. The sun was low in the sky. Our feet slipped slightly on small stones scattered on the asphalt driveway. The fact that I recall that detail intrigues me now.

Later, for some reason, I'm not sure why, I continue to draw this scene in my mind. I remember other things about the moment. For example, it occurred when I was a young man searching for something to do with my life. The troubled boys were also searching for something, developing their identities as they tried to overcome the past abuses and bad memories. But at that moment, I think we were hoping for hamburgers for dinner. It felt good at that particular time to be together. I was on top of my game as a child and youth care worker, which hadn't always been the case.

But I still want to know more. There is something about this scene that calls to me. I try to get it out of mind but can't. We were walking, yet the scene seems like a still-life drawing. As we moved forward, we were captured at a moment in time. Our presence, the rhythm of our gait, the geese flying overhead(I'm pretty sure it was fall), the time of day, the calls I can still hear from the other boys inside the building on their own search just before dinner, were all part of the scene.

Several years ago, motivated, and at times perhaps haunted, by reflections on experiences such as the one above I began to write (draw) and interpret vignettes (sketches), based on my experiences working with troubled youth. My goal was to increase my understanding of these experiences and to develop examples that I could use to teach youth work. Over time, the process evolved into a mixed genre method of qualitative inquiry and experimental autobiography that I call *Sketching* (Krueger, 1995; 2004; 2006).

While doing this, I learned from many others with similar ambitions. My friends, youth, favorite fiction writers, filmmakers, youth workers, poets, and scholars showed me how to write and interpret my sketches. Now I am ready to present what I have learned. In this book, I describe sketching as a method of reflexivity and share some of my sketches for others who might want to learn from my experience. All of the material is written with the assumption that readers will question, analyze, and critique it in relationship to their own experiences.

I begin in Chapter 1: *Pavilion* where I left off in my last book (Krueger, 2004) with a new version of a sketch that shows my youth and the influences that led to my becoming a youth worker. Then in Chapter 2 *Sketching Youth, Self, and Youth Work* I describe how sketching evolved, the process I used to draw and interpret the sketches, and the theoretical and conceptual foundations.

Chapter 3: *Youth Work Is,* offers a definition of youth work that has evolved over several years of sketching. Chapter 4: *My Presence in Cross Cultural Youth Work* is a recent reflection that has evolved from discussions in our field about power and critical race theory. Chapters 5: *The Team Meeting: A Three Act Play,* 6: *Self In Action,* and 7: *Motion, Stillness, Waiting, Anticipating and other Themes* are additional examples of how I write and use sketches to understand and learn youth work. I close with an Epilogue: *Death Writing, Bulls, and White Nights,* with two sketches from my autobiography.

For those readers unfamiliar with the term youth work (a.k.a. child and youth care work), this is the work of people who work directly with youth, roughly ages 10 to 21 in residential treatment centers, group homes, runaway shelters, after school programs, "the streets," community centers, churches, camps, and a number of other programs that generally occur inside and outside youths' homes. Youth workers (also known as child and youth care workers and a number of other titles) are people who do youth work. Their challenge is to form relationships and create opportunities to learn and grow together with youth.

Some of the work in this book has appeared in different versions in my earlier publications. The use of repetition and the adding of new insights are part of the way I learn from my sketches and the literature. Many of my sketches have been drawn literally dozens of times, each new draft revealing something new to me. Sketching, as a method of research, and my sketches in this regard are works in progress.

ACKNOWLEDGMENTS

The black and white sketches are the work of Suzanne Vandeboom my long time partner and friend. Her drawings and life were the inspiration for much of the work in this book. For examples of her paintings please see:
www.artvitae.com/vandeboom

Jasson, my son, of course, and Gerry Fewster, a friend and colleague, who I refer to often in the text, were big influences. Thanks also to all the youth workers in my classes and on the streets, who have taught me so much over the years. Woodland Pattern Book Center, a community and literary book store in the best sense, is appreciated for the opportunity to hear some of the finest poets and writers in the country while being surrounded by fine art and many excellent books from small presses.

PAVILION

...I run north along the frozen beaches of Lake Michigan. The sunbather is out, shielded from the wind by reflectors. I wave; he waves back. For a moment the two of us alone brave winter. I continue, lost in the rhythm of my gait...

JAZZ AND LAKE MICHIGAN

"*Milwaukee, 1957)* I can hear them talking.

"How did you feel when Father died?" my uncle asks my father.

"Like the boy in James Joyce's story about the dead priest, sad and relieved."

"It was different when Mother died, wasn't it?" my uncle asks.

"Yes, God forgive us if we ever lose the benignity she tried to instill in us," my father says.

"Yes, God forgive them, Verona," my mother sighs to my aunt.

They, my aunt, uncle, father, and mother, are in the kitchen of our second story flat on Milwaukee's Northwest Side, drinking cocktails. I'm in my bedroom—14 going on 15. It's about 11:00 p.m. My older brother is asleep in his bed across the room.

After the company is gone and the house is dark, I get dressed and go into the kitchen. Something moves. My father is dancing in the moonlight in the living room. Hidden from view, I watch as he moves in and out of the shadows from the elm branches that cathedral the narrow street in front of the house. He's wearing the shirt and tie he wore to the life insurance company he's worked at all his adult life. With his hands in his pockets and his pant legs raised, he shuffles his feet to the music in his head. When he turns toward the window, the moon shines on his face. He's smiling, but his eyes seem far away.

(1996) An old woman puts out her cigarette and enters the church with "The Glory of God and His Most Blessed Mother" carved in stone above the doorway. After mass, she comes across the street to the coffee shop where I'm writing at a table next to the window in the sunlight. Her face is painted with thick makeup, her eyes accented like the eyes of a doll or small girl.

"Hello," says the owner, a conversationalist, who is behind the counter.

1

"Hi." *She sits down on a stool and puts her cigarette on the lip of the glass ashtray.* "My girlfriend is coming this weekend."

"How nice."

"We were in the same club in high school. We're going to the beach."

The owner nods and fills another customer's cup.

She reaches for the cigarette, talks to herself out loud, "I'll get a new swim suit. Maybe we'll take my beach umbrella too."

"That's good," *a young woman seated a couple stools away says.*

"Oh, you probably got a two piece," *the old woman laughs.*

(1957) I grab the car keys off the kitchen table, tiptoe down the back stairs, take a deep breath of late August air, back the Dodge out of the garage, and creep between the rows of clapboard duplexes--the houses and people in them familiar from the steps I take to the grocery store and from games of kick the can.

At the end of the alley, I turn east. Burleigh Street is bathed in the humid, warm glow of lights. A single pigeon disappears beneath the hood of the car and reappears eyeball to eyeball with me before flying off. The playground where I shoot buckets and the cemetery where my brother taught me to drive pass on the left. Once I reach Lake Michigan, I park next to the pavilion, which sits on the bluffs like a balcony above nature's great symphony. I get out. No one else is here.

(Milwaukee, 1917) From the step of the car, my grandfather watches the last of passengers walk toward the station, their silhouettes intermittently reappearing in the steam and passing steel girders as the train pulls slowly toward the yards. Near the end of the platform he jumps off and cleans up in the washroom then he takes the trolley to his bungalow on the South Side. My grandmother, a thin stern-looking but loving German woman with spectacles and premature grey hair tied into a bun, greets him at the door. He looks handsome in his conductor's uniform. She's wearing her black dress with the white lace collar.

He kisses her on the cheek and takes off his jacket, which she hangs up for him. As usual, dinner is ready. Their sons, Will, 10 (my father), and Charles, 12, ate earlier and went out to play in the remaining daylight. She sits across from him at the dining room table and listens as he eats and talks about his trip to South Dakota. When she feels the time is right, she says, "The roof is leaking."

"I'll take a look at it tomorrow," *he says and puts a spoonful of mashed potatoes into his mouth. He hates housework.*

After dinner, still restless from his travels, he goes to the neighborhood pub and drinks a few beers with his German friends. Eventually, the conversation turns to the war. They speak in English. German, which only a few years ago was the primary language in the schools and around town, is rarely spoken anymore in public. President Wilson has stirred up anger and hatred in the U.S. against the "Huns" abroad and here.

When he gets home, he reads Nietzsche..."all philosophers have the failing of thinking man is now," *and falls asleep with the book in his lap.*

In the morning, after breakfast with his wife and two sons, he climbs on the roof to fix the leak. It's a nice day. He works at a steady pace above his boys' attic bedroom. In the distance, he can see the ships in the harbor and the cream brick buildings downtown that give the city its nickname, Cream City. As morning slides into afternoon and the sun sinks beneath the barren elms, he feels a slight chill...

(1957) With a path from the moon running across the black water to my feet and white-capped waves pounding the rocks along the shore beneath me, I repeat the word pavilion, "pavilion, pavilion, pavilion," until it loses meaning then drive down to the shore and park next to the rocks where one by one the waves can crash over the top, wash down the sides, and cocoon me in water with the lights from the ships on the horizon shining like diamonds through a film of distant dreams.

(1995) "...a site of linguistic self-consciousness and a point on the map of the modern world that may only be a projection of our desire to give our knowledge a shape that is foreign to or other than it. Above all it is a place that is named." I read Seamus Dean's explanation of Joyce's use of language to name place in the introduction to Penguin Books' 1993 edition of A Portrait of the Artist as a Young Man.

(1957) A few days later, Russo and I take the North Shore electric train to the jazz festival in Chicago. He has a brush haircut; I have a duck's tail. We're both wearing leather jackets. The landscape is a blur, an endless stream of farms and telephone poles. To pass the time I drum on my knees while he bums a cigarette.

(1990) "I'm thinking of getting my ear pierced like you," I say to my son, Devon, on the Charles Bridge in Prague shortly after the Velvet Revolution.

"You'll just look like a middle aged guy trying to be cool," he smiles and hands an earring back to a young woman sitting on a blanket.

We leave the bridge and walk past Kafka's father's store to a pub in Old Town where we are seated with two young Hungarian men. Devon speaks to them in French. One's a carpenter, the other a tailor. "They know where I can get a Soviet Army coat," Devon says.

"Go ahead, I'll meet you later on the bridge." After he leaves, I stay, have a sandwich then return to the bridge. The night sky is clear, the water calm. Behind me an old man is playing the accordion, his arms opening and closing the billows. I look at the castle where Vaclav Havel, the reluctant president, and playwright who wrote for the Theatre of the Absurd (and later as part of a liberation movement from a prison cell), lives, and wonder if he can still find time to write.

"What are you thinking?" The light is at Devon's back. He's wearing the long Soviet coat, his tall silhouette, faceless, his voice smooth, like the water that flows under the bridge.

"Nothing really. You look good in that coat."

3

(1957) There is a photo of my mother taken in the 1920s before she met my father, in the days when she smoked cigarettes, drove a Model T, and worked, a woman ahead of her times in those days. She is smiling coquettishly from beneath her flapper hat. The reflection I see in the train window on the moving countryside is that face. I comb my hair back into my duck's tail, jut my jaw out, and take a sideways glance trying to look older.

(1990) "My ageing was very sudden. I saw it spread over my features one by one, changing the relationship between them, making the eyes larger, the expression sadder, the mouth more final, leaving great creases in the forehead. But instead of being dismayed, I watched the process with the same interest I might have taken in the reading of a book. And I knew I was right, that one day it would slow down and take its normal course." I read in Harper and Row's 1985 edition (p.4) of Marguerite Duras', The Lover *while looking for a way to write my experiences.*

(1957) Slowly the farmland fades into brown-brick buildings then taller and taller buildings. From the train station, we walk inland. The city is like another planet: canyons of skyscrapers that block the sun, drunks, students, and businessmen all mixed together. We arrive at the Chicago Stadium early and toss coins with two other boys. Soon men in cardigan sweaters and women in evening gowns begin to arrive. Between us, Russo and I win a buck. By the time we finish, the stadium is almost full. We mill around, find our seats and wait. Eventually, the buzz of the crowd gives way to the mellow sound of Coleman Hawkins' saxophone followed by JJ Johnson, Dave Brubeck, and Ella Fitzgerald. When Miles Davis plays, he bends his head over his trumpet and turns his back to the crowd.

(2006) I listen to Bitches' Brew on the sound system in my new car.
"Why did you change direction at the height of your popularity," Miles was asked in an interview I heard somewhere, I think with Quincy Jones.
"Because I liked what I was playing too much," he said.
I turn up the sound.

Afterwards, still high on the music, we walk toward the lake. Outside a nightclub a woman with tassels on her tits is framed inside the cutout of a star.
"You boys aren't sixteen much less twenty-one," the doorman says to Russo.
Russo starts to argue. I pull him by the arm. On Michigan Avenue, he proclaims the Prudential building the tallest in the world. We cross the street into Grant Park. A bum hits us for a quarter. At the marina, a man with a torn jacket is fishing.
"Catch anything?" Russo asks.
"No, not yet," the man says. You can see his broken teeth when he talks.
"What you using?" I ask.
"Bacon."
"Bull," Russo says.

The man reaches in his jacket, pulls out a package wrapped in wax paper, unfolds the paper, and shows us the bacon.

"Never heard of that before," I say as the man puts the bacon back in his jacket.

The man looks at me. "Probably a lot of things you never heard of."

I turn my back to the lake like Miles Davis.

"Where you boys been?"

"At the jazz festival," I say proudly.

"No kidding. I used to play jazz."

"What instrument?" Russo asks.

"Piano."

"Where did you play?" I ask.

"All over."

"Why'd you stop?"

"Lost my timing."

(1997) A light is on upstairs in my former writing teachers house. Boxes can be seen in the window. The rest of the house is dark, the basement where she hanged herself among the old clothes and phonograph records, and the first floor, where sometimes when I sat across from her at the dining room table and read my work to her I could anticipate her response.

I used to make her laugh. It was easy. The slightest innuendo or hint of humor would set her off, in those days, when she laughed. She saw things where there wasn't anything. Always lurking, beneath the surface, there was something, for her, in a word or scene or image. Where I saw only a word or scene or image, she saw something more.

But like now, there was nothing, other than the sorrow, so I walk to the bookstore on the corner where I used to go after a lesson and page through books she recommended. The back of the jacket cover of Camus' first book, A Happy Death, *reads: "For here is the young Camus himself, in love with the sea and sun, enraptured by women, yet disdainful of romantic love, and already formulating the philosophy of action and moral responsibility that would make him central to the thought of our time..."*

(1957) On the way home, Russo falls asleep. I try not to look at my reflection as the jazz rhythms keep repeating in my head to the clickety-clack of the wheels.

"What are you doing taking a shower this time of night!" my mother knocks on the door.

I don't respond. I just stand under the hot water, trying to wash away the part of Chicago that touched The Lake.

(1994) "Certain things lie beyond my scope. I shall never understand the harder problems of philosophy. Rome is the limit of my traveling. As I drop asleep at night it strikes me that I shall never see savages in Tahiti spearing fish by the light of a blazing cresset ..." I lose myself in and try to grasp Virginia Woolf in the Harcourt Brace Jovanovich, 1959 edition of The Waves, *p. 186.*

(1957) A few days later, I take Nicole to Hell, a coffee shop for beats. She moved here this summer and wears a beret and vest, like the older girls. We sit on huge pillows and listen to Charlie Parker on large headphones. During a break, she puts her head on my shoulder.

"Do you like jazz?" she asks.

I tell her about the jazz festival and the man. She listens.

Later, we walk to the lake. I put my T-shirt on the ground in the shadows of the pavilion. She gets down on her back and raises her arms to me. It's my first time. I enter her and move back and forth the way Russo showed me. I'm too embarrassed to moan the way she does. Suddenly, my body stretches and explodes. She cries out as if she feels the same thing. Exhausted, I roll on my back and look at the stars.

(1976) "He climbed up the ladder and wondered if he had the strength to get home. He had done what he wanted. He had swum the county, but was so stupefied with exhaustion that his triumph seemed vague." I read these lines from The Swimmer *by John Cheever in a Vintage Book collection of his stories, see the movie later with Burt Lancaster, vow never to live in the suburbs, and become fascinated with stories about men with something at the edge of their consciousness, like in a Sam Shepard play.*

"Let's go for a swim," she says after we rest a few minutes.

Clothes in hand, we walk naked down the steps in front of the pavilion and climb over the rocks to the water. She puts her arms around my neck and lets her naked body dangle against mine. In the cold water, it feels good, almost better than before, less scary. When she lets go, I swim as far out as I can, head turned up at the bright stars, then down into the black water, as if the light and dark are connected to the movement of my arms and legs.

Rungs

(1961) Near the end of my youth, I hitchhike to New Orleans. One night I meet an older woman with dark hair in Preservation Hall. We pass her flask back and forth.

"Com'on, don't pass out on me," she says on Bourbon Street.

We climb the stairs to her apartment and fuck under her ceiling fan.

(1965) "He closed his eyes, surrendering himself to her, body and mind, conscious of nothing in the world but the dark pressure of her softly parting lips. They pressed upon his brain as upon his lips as though they were the vehicle of vague speech; and between them he felt the unknown and timid pressure, darker than the swoon of sin, softer than the sound of odour," I read for the first time from A Portrait of the Artist as a Young Man.

(1961) In the morning, with booze and sweat seeping from a black hole deep inside me, I run through The Quarter to St Charles Boulevard. On and on I run until among the mansions, until word and image come together to create something at the edge of my consciousness, something too beautiful or perhaps too painful to touch.

(1950) I pose, bent sideways at the waist with my ribs protruding and my arms stretched up the shaft of an oar, and wait for my mother to shoot a photo so I can row around the raft of our two week vacation "up north" on a small lake. It starts to rain. I run to the fort my brother and I built in the woods. As water drips on my head, the branches piled on the ceiling of the fort feel like tentacles of holiday's end twisting through me.

(1967) One by one they empty their pockets. Zip guns, switchblades, and brass knuckles fall into the metal garbage can that the sergeant drags along the middle of the floor of the barracks at Fort Ord California. Nothing to offer, I remain at attention.

(1978) I stand in front of the floor length mirror and rehearse my first speech. For six months, over and over again I repeat the words while looking at myself afraid I will forget what to say. I fly to Philadelphia and stand exposed to 500 youth workers. It is as if I am speaking back to myself, catching the words like a robot, regurgitating what has been stored on my tape, exposed for all, yet none to see, drifting over the audience, the words a beat to a song outside me, the movement more important than the meaning.

Night falls. Mist from the ocean drifts through the open windows carrying the spinal meningitis, which already killed two draftees, inland like the sickness of preparation for a war that I could no longer avoid, my special student status having run out, my draft number high, and my desire to leave my life in Milwaukee for Canada not strong enough. I get out of bed, leave the barracks, climb the fence to the Pacific Ocean, and sit on the beach, thinking about Lake Michigan.

... As rafts of ice sit motionless a few yards off shore, I continue north lost in the rhythm of my gait. Ahead, a man is standing on the beach behind a white door, facing the lake with his head and shoulders visible through the square opening where the glass used to be. He's wearing a black turtleneck and black knit seaman's hat. A few yards away, another man is standing behind a tripod. The sky is deep blue, the ground white, and the water, black.

Near the water purification plant, I enter a ravine that rises to the pavilion. Surrounded by the bluffs, it is a quiet, private place. I rest a moment where the sun shines through the branches, and listen to melting snow trickle towards the lake, then run up the steps two at a time and look down into the cold water I once swam in on a warm summer night...

7

The next day they cut our hair. We all look the same. I keep my mouth shut, and do my duty--run and shoot, swing through the rungs of the overhead ladder like a monkey before meals, and cover my ears from the artillery blasts, the way I did firecrackers as a boy. At the end of the day, when all is finally quiet, I fall asleep listening to jazz in my head.

While the regulars are sent for more combat training, I'm sent to the Mojave desert to work with linemen. High on a pole the desert seems like a vast sea. At midday the heat hums in the wire like a poisonous insect and the smog drifts in from Los Angeles. All I want to do is put in my time and get it over with, but in my dreams, I can see their blood on the rungs of the overhead ladder we swung through before dinner, blood from the hands of the poor boys from the city where the judge said, "Jail or the Army?" the poor boys who will go to fight the war, while I, a reservist, will go home to serve out my time on weekends.

When I can't sleep, I walk in the desert. It so quiet I can hear the jackrabbits running. On and on I walk, one foot after the other hitting the ground, like the man I will see years later in the opening to the movie *Paris Texas.* In these moments, war and politics aren't my concern, stillness is.

(1972) "A Tuesday," an elderly gentleman says, as I walk him across the county mental institution grounds where I volunteered to serve out the rest of my reserve time one weekend a month.

I just gave him a date in the last hundred years I picked out of the blue. I can give him any date during that time period, like say June 12th 1915, and he, a savant, can immediately give me the day of the week.

"Give me another one, go ahead, any day," he says, happy I think to be outdoors away from the benches where many of the patients have developed cricks in their necks from sitting and sleeping for hours drugged.

(1968) Jobless, going from one bar to another, I see a young woman standing on a bus stop. She has long brown hair and beautiful eyes.

"Hello," I say.

She smiles, turns away.

"Where are you going?"

"Home for the weekend."

"What's in there?"

"Drawings. I'm an artist."

"Do you go to the University?"

"Yes."

"Where do you live?"

"Up north, I'm going to the Greyhound station."

"I'll give you a ride."

She looks at me, pauses, picks-up her portfolio. "Okay."

"Mark," I say.

"Suzanne."

On the way downtown she draws something in the fog on the window.

"When did you know you wanted to be an artist?" I ask.

"It's all I ever wanted to be."

She returns the next day and moves in with me.

"See the cardinal?" she asks a few days later as we walk along the bluffs in the park.

"Where?"

"In the tree. It's bright red."

"I'm partially color blind."

She smiles, puts her hands on my head, and gently turns it toward a branch in a tree. "See there?"

"Yes," I pretend.

We sit under a tree. "Do you ever think there are no words for feelings?" I ask.

"Yes, that's why I paint."

"But images, like words, are symbols. Do you ever think images aren't enough?"

"I don't think much when I paint."

That evening she gives me a drawing of a naked man crouched in a beam of light. He's bald with long, lean muscles and sunken eyes, and does not cast a shadow in the light at his feet. I hang it at the head of my bed. In the morning, her gentle breaths fall in steady beats on my chest.

"I left my body once," she says.

"When?"

"I was fourteen and in the bathtub and suddenly I left my body," she starts to cry.

"Why did you leave?"

"Because I didn't belong there. Not in that body in that house."

"So what happened?"

She wipes away her tears. "I was changed forever. I knew I could survive and that I had to leave home. I never told anyone this."

"I'm glad you told me."

"Suzanne takes you down to a place near the river... You can hear the boats go by, you can spend the night beside her, and you know that she is half crazy that's why you want to be there...she feeds you tea and oranges that come all the way from China, and just when you mean to tell her that you have no love to give her, she gets you on her wave length, she lets the river answer that you've always been her lover... and you want to travel with her, and you want to travel blind and you know that she will trust you, for you've touched her perfect body with your mind...

...and Jesus was a sailor when he walked upon the water and he spent a long time watching from his lonely wooden tower and when he knew for certain only drowning men could see him he said all men will be sailors then until the sea shall

free them and he himself was broken long before the sky was open... forsaken almost human he sank beneath your wisdom like a stone...

Suzanne takes your hand, she leads you to the river, she is wearing rags and feathers from salvation army counters and the sun falls down like honey on our lady of the harbor and she shows you where to look now upon the garbage and the flowers and there are heroes in the seaweed and there are children in the morning, they are leaning out for love now and they'll lean that way forever while Suzanne holds the mirror... and you want to travel with her and you want to travel blind and you know that she will trust you for she has touched your perfect body with her mind..." From Leonard Cohen's Suzanne.

Summer passes quickly. After a short interview, I'm hired at the residential center for troubled boys. Daniel, 14, arrives a few weeks later. I greet him in the waiting room. He's alone.

"Daniel?"

He gets up from his chair and approaches, his T- shirt tattered and his face wind-burned from several days on the streets.

"Mark." I hold out my hand.

He glares at me, continues walking. I walk alongside and motion for him to enter an office.

"Hi Daniel, I'm Marjorie, your therapist." Marjorie, a new, young therapist, holds out her hand...another glare.

"Before Mark takes you upstairs I want to tell you a little about our program," Marjorie says.

"I don't give a fuck about the program!" He grabs a paperweight from her desk, throws it at her, and takes a swing at me. I duck and grab him around the waist and quick-step behind him remembering my supervisor, Ernie's, instructions: "Grab both arms by the wrist and cross them in front of him, then put your knee behind his knee and dip like a basketball player taking the leap out of a re-bounder in front of him, and collapse together to the floor. If he's small enough (Daniel just barely is) sit him in front of you with your legs hooked over his so he can't kick, his body cradled in your arms and your head tight to his so he can't butt you. Then prepare for a long wait. It helps to have something to support your back."

"Marjorie, would you move that couch over here." My voice shakes. She gets on one end of the couch and pushes until it's between my back and the wall. He twists like a dog trying to avoid a bath. "Your mother sucks cock! Your ol' lady sleeps with horses, cops, pigs!" The veins in his neck cord and his body strains like a stretched bow.

My arms ache. Daniel rests, then jerks like a fish out of water, rests and jerks again. Gradually he gives up and the tension subsides. We sit quietly, soaked in sweat, limbs intertwined, breaths as if coming from the same set of lungs.

(1971) Beads separate the bedroom from the living room in our small attic apartment. She works on the floor beneath the skylight crouched over her canvas like a butterfly on a daisy, the work an extension of her. After she goes to sleep, I

listen to Sweet Baby Jane, Fire and Rain on the reel-to-reel tape player, her work beyond my reach.

In summer, Devon pretzels out between her legs with double joints and a slight case of jaundice, looking just like the painting she did beforehand: the moonchild with cream eyelids and lashes of fine sable hair. While she breastfeeds him, I walk on the breakwater that separates the lake from the inner harbor.

Several years later, on a quiet summer afternoon in my cabin on a small lake, I reflect while reading again from the Harcourt Brace Jovanovich 1959 edition of Virginia Woolf's, The Waves: "Thus, when I come to shape here at this table between my hands of the story of my life and set it before you as a complete thing, I have to recall things gone far, gone deep, sunk into this life or that, become part of it; dreams too, things surrounding me, and the inmates, those old half-articulated ghosts who keep up their hauntings by day and night, who utter their confused cries, who put out their phantom fingers and clutch at me as I try to escape— shadows of people one might have been, unborn selves..."

"I'm going to let go of your left arm then your right one." Step by step, I release my hold until Daniel is standing across from me, showing no remorse. Certain that he has won, whatever there is to win, I wipe my nose.

"Are you okay?" Marjorie asks.

"Yes, I'll be fine."

I take him upstairs. "Sticky suckers," Suzanne calls the smell of urine and disinfectant that I take home at night in my clothes and hair. It reminds me of the way my father used to try to cover the booze with mouthwash and Old Spice aftershave, a trick that never worked. At the top of the stairs, I part the fire doors. The other boys are in school.

"Your room is down the hall," I say. He walks to my side, runs his shoulder along the wall.

A grocery bag with his things is on the bed. He digs through it. "Bastards," he says. Ernie searches all the new boys things for drugs and weapons. Daniel takes out a T-shirt and pair of jeans, starts to change, then looks at me, "Mind."

I give him a moment to change and unpack, wait outside the door with my back to the wall and question what I'm doing here. I don't know why, but for some reason I feel at home.

When I re-enter, Daniel is sitting at the desk with a photo.

"Who's that?"

"None of your fuckin' business."

I don't respond.

"My sister."

"She's nice looking.... What's this one?"

"None of your business." He puts the photos in the drawer, and asks, "Why do you work here?"

"I'm not sure."

11

CHAPTER 1

(2001) "The same or almost the same points were always being approached afresh from different directions and new sketches made. Very many of these were badly drawn or uncharacteristic, marked by all the defects of a weak draftsman. And when they were rejected a number of tolerable ones were left, which now had to be rearranged and cut down, so that if you looked at them you could get a picture of a landscape. Thus the book is really only an album." I read this passage *in the preface to* Philosophical Investigations *(Wittgenstein, 2001, pages unmumbered).*

"So you can get your jollies, probably," Daniel says.
"Want a coke?" I ask.
He nods and we walk to the day room.
I keep an eye on him as I buy cokes from the vending machine, then we sit across from one another at a small table. He sips his coke, looks down, then up.
"Your shoes untied." He stares at me.
I stare back.

Pavilion (Def): A temporary shelter; the external ear, place as is the place that is one's self

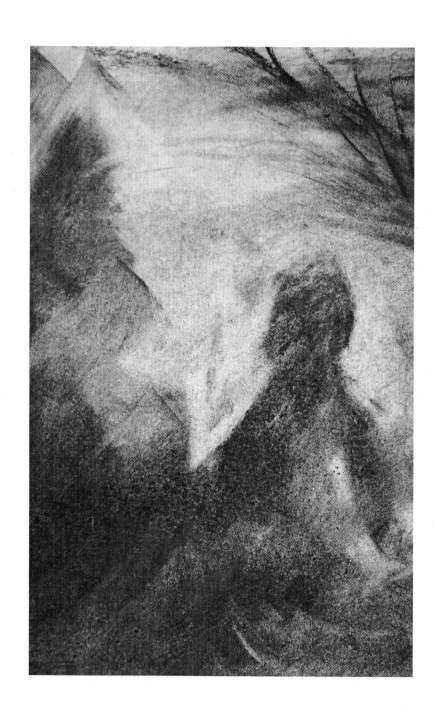

CHAPTER 2

SKETCHING YOUTH, SELF, AND YOUTH WORK

The 2000 edition of the *Handbook of Qualitative Research* (Denzin & Lincoln, 2000) showed qualitative research in a period of ferment and explosion, which was defined by breaks from the past, a focus on previously silent voices, and a concern with moral discourse, with critical conversations about democracy race, gender, class, nation, freedom, and community. As evidenced in many of the chapters in this and the following anthology (Denzin & Lincoln, 2005), researchers and practitioners used a variety of methods to understand human experiences. Some of them mixed literary, poetic, journalistic, fictional, cinematic, documentary, factual and ethnographic writing and representation. All were concerned to some degree with the "what is" and the ways it could be shown. The researcher "looked into" an experience, and tried to show it in a way that was consistent with the way that it was felt, heard, and/or visualized.

Sketching was developed in this spirit. My goal was to understand and show my experiences, as I did a moment ago in, *Pavilion*. I blended together what I had learned from creative writing, qualitative inquiry, philosophy, youth work, and whatever else I could get my hands on to help me look into and hear youth, self, and youth work in reflection. In this chapter, I show how sketching evolved as a method of reflexivity, and, in the process, I try to make myself visible as a researcher who is at the center of researching his experience.

BACKGROUND

Most of my life, I have been experiencing, studying, and learning about youth (adolescence), first as a youth, then as a youth worker, and now as a professor of youth work. I am fascinated with youth as a continuous part of life. Not so much the "good old days" of youth, but rather youth as a significant period of development and growth that forever changes the way we feel and see the world around us--the youth that we carry with us as adults and that continues to enrich and inform our lives.

The youth that began in the days when we had new sexual feelings, thought more about what people thought about us, and struggled with the answer to the question, "who am I?" The years and moments when we chased windmills, like Don Quixote one moment, and turned inward, like Hamlet, the next. The part of us that continually explores Derrida's notion of the "who or what?" Do I want to be loved for who I am (the singular me) and/or what I am (what I do, how I look, etc.)? And the exhaustion, energy, resilience, motion, waiting, anticipating, questioning, and becoming that is part of the journey.

I am also interested in youth who are troubled and/or at risk, youth that are put at jeopardy by societies, communities, and families that neglect and abuse them. The ways these youths make meaning and fight and claw their way through life, and the things that can be done to fill their stories with moments of connection, discovery, and empowerment.

Interrelated with this is my interest in youth work (a.k.a. child and youth care work), or the work people do to care for youth, the ways youth workers are with youth and promote their development in the lived experience. Finally, I am also interested in the self as is manifest in interactions between youth workers and youth, and/or the history of youth that workers bring to these moments that helps them know and understand what they are doing.

My Youth

My learning about adolescence, and subsequently the foundations for sketching, started in my youth in Milwaukee in the 1950s and 1960s as just seen in *Pavilion* Briefly I was the son of German parents, who like most Germans in Milwaukee, had abandoned their heritage during two world wars, worked hard, and moved from poverty into the mainstream middle class. We had become you might say part of what author Phillip Roth described in his Pulitzer Prize winning novel as the *American Pastoral.*

For my parents this was a major achievement, but for me it created a lifestyle that I often felt was boring and sterile, so I tried to escape from the pastoral. With others of my generation, I tried to find myself in an era of beats and hippies who I both wanted to emulate and be different than. I had sex, drank, did drugs, and got into trouble.

Near the end of my youth, I hitchhiked to New Orleans and was awakened in a world of jazz and a foreign, rich culture that was unlike anything I had experienced. When I returned I finished my undergraduate work at the University of Wisconsin in the 1960s, joined the Army Reserves to avoid the draft, protested, and floundered around until I met a beautiful artist on a street corner. We moved in together the next day. I was 26 and she was only 19, but her sense of certainty about her work, and awareness of her feelings amazed me.

Finding a Home: Becoming a Youth Worker

Shortly after I met Suzanne, a friend recommended that I apply for an opening at a residential treatment center for boys. This appealed to me because a few years earlier I had worked on the playgrounds with youth during the summer. After a short interview, I accepted the position and was "thrown to the wolves." Without much preparation or supervision, I was put on the unit with four other workers and 36 aggressive, angry, frightened and very sad boys. Almost from the beginning, however, I felt at home (Krueger, 2003). There was something about the pace, struggle, and play that told me this was where I had to be, an existential hum perhaps that called to me and told me that this was where I would learn about my *self* as well as the youth.

I also learned in those years what it meant to be troubled beyond the troubling experiences that were part of most adolescent's lives. The boys at the center had been victims of terrible and sometimes unthinkable abuse and neglect. Some had been in trouble with the law, others were just too much for their parents or a foster family to handle. When I read their case histories it put my own youth into a different context. I often said to myself, "I'd be a basket case if I'd gone through that" and marveled at their resilience.

It was, of course, a gut wrenching, tough, demanding, emotionally painful and sometimes extremely frustrating job. It was also fun and good, hard work. My colleagues and I, in *Mash*-like (*Mash* was a movie and a T.V. series in the U.S.) fashion, were dedicated to our tasks during our shifts, and full of humor and mischief afterwards as we reflected and tried to "come down" from a long day. I had the good fortune to work with a group of committed, energetic workers at a time in U.S. history (late 1960s and 1970s) when working with youth was perhaps more valued in society. For us I know it was more than an occupation, it was our cause. Together in our innocence we were going to, excuse the language "change the fucking world" for youth. When I got home I felt I had been in the thick of something important, a place in which I had to be sincere and genuine in order to succeed.

Everyday the teenage boys, who had become experts (on conscious and unconscious levels) at spotting fakes and liars, taught me something about how to "walk the talk" and "be real." They seemed to have antennae that let them know a behavior was out of synch with a feeling, or words were incongruent with actions, and they would tell us with their words and/or confronting or evasive behavior. I tried to use what I learned from them about being present and genuine with my own son, and to make sure he didn't end up troubled even though I knew that what he became would be his choice.

Many of the skills and attitudes that later shaped my research were honed in those years. I learned, for example, how to hear, read, smell, and see--sometimes with eyes in the back of my head--and to interpret their stories and actions. I also sensed, perhaps more than knew, that in order to understand youth I had to be *with* them *in* the moment learning from and about self. Later in my career, a pivotal book in this regard was, *Being in Child Care: A Journey into Self* (Fewster, 1990).

Moving Toward Narrative and Story

About eight years after I started working as a youth worker, I decided to go back to school. I wanted to understand and learn as much as I could about youth while I continued to work with them. Unlike my earlier undergraduate experience at the University of Wisconsin in the 1960s, when I didn't know what I wanted to be or where I was going, my graduate learning was one exciting revelation after another. The theory and facts of adolescence were enriched by my experience as a youth worker and vice versa.

During my doctoral studies, I developed a center at the university to research and teach youth work. Our goal was to improve youth work in our country, and in some small way to help change the communities in which youth were growing up. My dissertation was a qualitative analysis of teamwork. For a year, I sat in team meetings at residential treatment centers studying how youth workers made, and followed through with, their decisions. After that I became an assistant professor, taught youth work, did both qualitative and quantitative research, and wrote books about practice techniques and social conditions for youth, including *Intervention Techniques for Child and Youth Care Workers* and *Careless to Caring for Troubled Youth.*

To make my work accessible and show it in context, I developed case examples and vignettes to exemplify key points. I was good at and enjoyed this part of the process. It seemed like a natural way to write about the work. In these narratives I could once again see, feel, hear, and smell youth work the way I recalled it as an imperfect process of interaction that was enriched and fraught with all the success, failure, struggle, joy, sadness, and discovery that were part of being human. Then one day, a creative writing professor who had an office next to mine encouraged me to try a novel. I took up her challenge and was immediately hooked.

The novel, *Floating* (Krueger, 1987), which was based on my earlier experience as a youth worker, (we were called child and youth care workers then) was well received in my field and used in classrooms to teach child and youth care work. One reviewer, Henry Maier, a mentor and expert on adolescent development, said that the characters were internally and externally consistent, and that he would use it instead of his own textbook in his classes. This meant a lot to me.

I included the novel in my portfolio for tenure because I felt it was my best work to date. When challenged by my university colleagues about its scholarship, I made a somewhat naive but classic argument, which was that it had relevance the way *Moby Dick* had relevance, as a precursor to psychoanalytic theory. In story, if properly told, you could see and feel the human conditions in which theory was experienced, and from which new theory was about to evolve. I got tenured and followed the first novel with another novel, *In Motion,* and a book of my first sketches, *Buckets: Sketches From a Youth Worker's Log Book.*

To enrich my work, I read and reread literature, and learned about youth in reflection, portraiture, and lost innocence in books such as James Joyce's *A Portrait of the Artist as a Young Man* and Marguerite Duras' *The Lover.* Being a few more years removed from my own chronological youth provided new insight as I reread *Catcher in the Rye.* Life experience and biography also showed me with some disappointment that writers like Kerouac and Hemingway used lyricism and repetition perhaps to hide a deeper confusion of and incongruence with youth. The way these authors lived their lives outside their fiction: the unintentional lies, internal inconsistencies and fantasies of youth perhaps.

In my classes, we wrote, interpreted, and shared stories about youth, our own and others. We also watched and interpreted films and documentaries, including, *Hoop Dreams, Boys in the Hood, What's Eating Gilbert Grape*, and more recently *Dog Town and the Z Boys, Ghost World, Thirteen, and Raising Victor Vargas*. Films and documentaries like these put youth work in context. A film buff since my youth, it was also an extension of my growing interest in montage as an expression of the lived experience.

Vignettes and Postmodernism: The First Sketches

During this period of watching films, reading literature, and writing and interpreting stories, I became interested in the growing body of postmodern thought that argued we built and shaped ourselves into the world through unique cultural, familial, and communal experiences, and that our meanings and realities were constantly changing as we interacted and our narratives evolved (Bruner, 1990). This was affirming because it was consistent with the way I experienced life and the way my mind worked, but it also reinforced a growing concern that something was still missing.

My reflections didn't really come to me in stories with a beginning, plot and a climax. They came to me in short bursts of thought juxtaposed with other short bursts of thought. I made meaning from a montage of experiences, the way I think youth often make meaning. Sven Birkerts (2006, p. 4) described this process of reflection in his introduction to a special issue on memoir of *Cream City Review*, a literary journal by referring to Nobokov words at the beginning of *Speak Memory,* "In probing my childhood (which is the next best thing to probing eternity). I see the awakening of consciousness as a series of spaced flashes, with the intervals between them diminishing until bright blocks of perception are formed, affording memory a slippery hold."

Also, as in Proust's *Remembrance of Things Past*, time in reflection spiraled forward and back with key experiences showing up in different places and taking on new meanings with each appearance. So I began to draw, question, interpret, and juxtapose (as shall be described in more detail later in this chapter) several versions of sketches such as the following sketch, which was part of *Pavilion*, derived from the opening to *Floating* and repeated here, that for one reason or another seemed to have a significant meaning and impact my understanding of the work:

Basket Hold

Shortly after I begin work at a residential center for boys, Daniel, 14, arrives. I greet him in the waiting room. He's sitting alone, elbows on his knees, chin on his hands.
"Daniel?"

Without responding, he gets up from his chair and approaches, his T-shirt tattered and his face wind-burned from several days on the streets.

"Mark." I hold out my hand.

He glares at me, continues walking. I walk alongside and motion for him to enter an office.

"Hi Daniel, I'm Marjorie, your therapist." Marjorie, a new, young therapist, holds out her hand.

Another glare.

"Before Mark takes you upstairs I wanted to tell you a little about our program," Marjorie says.

"I don't give a fuck about the program!" he grabs a paperweight from her desk, throws it at her, and takes a swing at me. I duck and grab him around the waist and quick-step behind him remembering my supervisor, Ernie's, instructions:

"Grab both arms by the wrist and cross them in front of him, then put your knee behind his knee and dip like a basketball player taking the leap out of a re-bounder in front of him, and collapse together to the floor. If he's small enough, (Daniel just barely is) sit him in front of you with your legs hooked over his so he can't kick, his body cradled in your arms and your head tight to his so he can't butt you. Then prepare for a long wait. It helps to have something to support your back."

"Marjorie, would you move that couch over here." My voice shakes. She gets on one end of the couch and pushes until it's between my back and the wall. He twists like a dog trying to avoid a bath. "Your mother sucks cock! Your ol' lady sleeps with horses, cops, pigs!" The veins in his neck cord and his body strains like a stretched bow. There is a pause then he starts again. Marjorie gets down and holds his feet.

My arms ache. Daniel rests, then jerks like a fish out of water, rests and jerks again until gradually he gives up, and the tension subsides, and we sit quietly, soaked in sweat, limbs inter-twined, breaths as if coming from the same set of lungs.

In this sketch, which is based on an experience early in my career, I was trying to capture and understand a first encounter with a boy with whom I would eventually develop a positive relationship. Prior to his placement, the boy, like most of the boys at the center, had been abused. I knew at the time if I could hold him safely without hurting him there was a chance he could begin to trust me. But he was making it very difficult.

"I'm going to let go of your left arm then your right one." Step by step I release my hold until Daniel is standing across from me, showing no remorse. Certain that he has, won whatever there is to win, I wipe my nose.

"Are you okay?" Marjorie asks.

"Yes, I'll be fine."

I take him upstairs. "Sticky suckers," Suzanne calls the smell of urine and disinfectant that I take home at night in my clothes and hair. It reminds me of the way my father used to try to cover the booze with mouthwash and Old Spice aftershave, a trick that never worked. At the top of the stairs, I part the fire doors. The other boys are in school.

"Your room is down the hall," I say. He walks to my side, runs his shoulder along the wall.

A grocery bag with his things is on the bed. He digs through it. "Bastards," he says. Ernie searches all the new boys' things for drugs and weapons. Daniel takes out a T-shirt and pair of jeans, starts to change, then looks at me, says "Mind."

I give him a moment to change and unpack, wait outside the door with my back to the wall and question what I'm doing here. I don't know why but for some reason I feel at home.

When I re-enter, Daniel is sitting at the desk with a photo.

"Who is that?"

"None of your fuckin' business."

I don't respond.

"My sister."

"She's nice looking.... What's this one?"

"None of your business." He puts the photos in the drawer and asks, "Why do you work here?"

"I'm not sure."

"So you can get your jollies, probably," Daniel says.

"Want a coke?" I ask.

He nods and we walk to the day room.

I keep an eye on him as I buy cokes from the vending machine, then we sit across from one another at a small table. He sips his coke, looks down, then up.

"Your shoes untied." He stares at me.

I stare back.

While drawing and interpreting this sketch, I asked questions such as: Why was Daniel angry? Why was he there? Did he belong? Why didn't he feel he belonged? What was it about the place, him, me, us, his past that told him to get out of there? Who was I in those moments, and why was I there? What was I thinking when we stared at each other? A young man myself, was I trying to prove myself to Marjorie, a young woman? How did he and I interpret this physical contact in relationship to our previous physical contacts? Let's assume he was black. I am white. How did our temperament, personalities, cultures, and histories influence the restraint and actions afterwards? And of course what were all the other issues associated with power, race, control, gender, role models, etc.? Perhaps most importantly, the sketch shows and raises questions about our fears, vulnerabilities, self-doubt and uncertainty as human beings at the beginning of a new relationship. Even today I am curious about what was loaded into that stare—a question I will try to answer in more detail in following chapters. Since this initial sketch, Daniel, who is the main character in *Floating* and was based on two boys I once worked with has become a main character in subsequent sketches and investigations. In this regard, I often also think of him as a muse and a reflection of myself as manifest in my characterizations and interpretations.

21

Fiction

Early on, I decided not to make my sketches exact replicas of my experiences, but rather representations that rang true with my experiences. I knew I could not remember the experiences exactly as they occurred, and that the meaning had changed with time. (Bruner, 1990). Thinking of my sketches as fictions also gave me greater leeway to express myself, as Richardson (2000) suggested when she wrote, "Staging qualitative research as fiction frees the author from some constraints, protects the author from criminal or other charges and may protect the identities of those studied (p. 933)."

Making the case for fiction writing as research in human service was tricky business in an academic environment. I understood this. Nonetheless, it was the direction in which I knew I had to go if I wanted to research my experience the way I had experienced and could best express it. In recent years, I have been pleased to find a considerable amount of support for this decision from other researchers with similar feelings (Clough, 2002; Rambo Ronai, 1998, Sparks, 2002). I also learned that there has been a long history of using this approach. In her reflections on portraiture, a qualitative method that was the subject of a special issue of *Qualitative Inquiry,* Lawrence-Lightfoot (2005) wrote:

The intersection of fiction and social science has occurred since at least the 18th century when the two approaches to the study of life began to emerge from similar impulses and to express common themes…Novelists and social scientists began to strive for a closeness to life, seeking to capture the texture and nuance of human experience (p. 6).

Today in the debate about whether or not fiction is relevant research I subscribe to arguments like the following from Denzin:

I have no desire to reproduce arguments concerning the importance of maintaining some distinction between fictional (literary) and nonfictional (journalism, ethnography) texts. Nor do I distinguish among literary, nonliterary, fictional and nonfictional textual forms. They are too often used to police certain transgressive writing forms, such as fictional ethnographies. There is only narrative--that is, only different genre-defined ways of representing and writing about experiences and their multiple realities. The discourses of the postmodern world constantly intermingle literary, poetic, journalistic, fictional, cinematic, documentary, factual and ethnographic writing and representation. No form is privileged over the other; all simply perform a different function for a writer and an interpretive community (Denzin, 2001, p. 7).

Thus, my goal was to write sketches that were "true in the stories that contained them" (Denzin (2001, p. 153) and shed new light on my topic of inquiry. "I wanted the written pieces to convey the authority, wisdom, and perspective of the subjects, but I wanted them to feel as I had felt that the portrait might not look like them but somehow managed to reveal their essence" (Lawrence-Lightfoot, 2005, p. 6).

THE PROCESS

When I sketched, I was engaged in a non linear, sometimes circular process of selecting an experience, projecting myself into it, drawing it out out, interpreting it, juxtaposing it with other sketches, interpreting it again, and working the material over and over until it crystallized (Richardson, 2000, pp 934-935). The process of going back and forth, working and reworking, and interpreting along the way until a sketch rang true with an experience seemed as, if not more important than the product.

I'm not sure why I chose certain sketches over others. As I described in the Introduction, there was usually something that called me to a moment or scene, such as in the *Basket Hold* sketch presented earlier, which I have returned to over and over again. Sometimes I selected an experience that fit with a topic of investigation, such as presence, a theme described in the next chapter, and/or an experience that frequently showed up in my random reflections on youth work and my life, and for that reason alone seemed important.

Once I selected something to sketch, I tried to be present in the moment again. I took a breath, and tried to look and listen the way I learned to listen and look in youth work, sometimes with "eyes in the back of my head." Then once I felt I captured the moment I started to draw (write). Following what I learned from creative writing and a narrative form of counseling youth (Fay, 1989), I drew free hand at first to free myself of inhibitions, and/or to listen to the subconscious (free association).

I went over and over a sketch until it looked, moved, sounded, and felt right to me (rang true). It was as if I was using an eraser, much the way Suzanne drew with charcoal pencils, fingers, and eraser while enmeshed in her work. Rambo-Ronai (1998, p. 409), who developed her own method of sketching, used a similar analogy from her drawing class to describe how she had learned to draw and erase rapidly, working and reworking a sketch in her research. I wrote knowing that I would go through several drafts before I captured my scene the way it looked in my minds eye. Writing in this regard became a process of knowing and research (Richardson, 1994), the drafting as informative as the final product--knowing how to let go as important as knowing what to hold on to.

Making a Sketch Ring True

To validate a sketch, or make it ring true, I learned techniques from qualitative inquiry, such as thick and thin description and interpretation (Denzin, 2001), and crystallization as described by Richardson (2000), who, in making the case against triangulation, argued that there are many more than three sides to look at in human interactions (p. 934). I also borrowed a quote from a note card that short story writer Raymond Carver kept above his desk. The quote belonged to poet Ezra

Pound: "Fundamental accuracy of statement is the sole morality of writing (Carver, 1983, p. 21)." I read this as meaning each sentence and word had to be as accurate as possible, and the only way to get there was through work, hard work, the way serious writers like Flaubert, Pound, and Carver worked as they searched over and over for the words to describe people, places, and dialogue in their stories and poems.

Anthropologist Sarris (1993), in his investigation into the life of a Pomo Indian medicine woman, wrote about how important it was to be present and to speak across the spaces of their experiences searching for a mutual reality. In youth work and sketching, I tried to do the same. With the awareness that each participant in an interaction with me had a different story and way of looking at the world, I asked them or myself, "This is what its like for me. What's it like for you?" or "Tell me how you see it, I'm curious."

A technique I learned from my creative writing teacher was to read my work a loud. I would write a chapter or story and read it aloud to her as I sat across from her at her dining room table. After a while it got so that I could anticipate her response, which would signal when I wasn't being internally consistent, lost my rhythm, was out of touch with my character, or I had not achieved "fundamental accuracy of statement "(Carver, 1984 p. 100).

More often than not, I would turn to poets and good fiction writers when I was looking for tips to make my sketches ring true. They seemed to have a special way of seeing that evoked in me an "ah ha" experience. They invited me into their experiences rather than imposed them on me. Thus, I would look for advice from people like the great German Poet Rilke (1984), who in his classic book *Letters to a Young Poet* (one of the best sources on writing and life ever written), advised the new poet to write to please self, not some imaginary audience of magazine readers. I also learned from Rilke's experience. When he lost his way and stopped writing poetry for a while, he confided in his friend the sculptor Rodin, who told Rilke to go to the zoo and to look at the animals with two or three weeks not being to long to look at one animal (Bly, 1981, p. 129). The result was Rilke's seeing poems, the most famous being *The Panther* (Bly, 1981, p. 139) in which he powerfully captured the essence of a caged panther. So when I got stumped, I looked again into my experiences with the dream that I might see just one moment or scene with that depth.

I admired minimalist writers, like Camus, Hemingway, Chekhov, and Marguerite Duras. Their description, dialogue, and action always seemed to move the story forward, rather than bog it down. Beneath the simplicity was a considerable amount of complexity. Thus, I tried to strike out anything that wasn't needed to advance my sketches, with the hope that I would reveal the simplicity (thickness) on the other side of complexity. In hindsight, it might be said that I preferred thin description to thick description (Brekhus, Galliher, & Gurbrium, 2005) which I felt obscured the point by talking around it, or was sometimes used by researchers to impress rather than describe.

Interpretation

Often, I broke a sketch down to almost nothing (deconstructed), then started again looking for what belonged, and didn't belong, while comparing my work to what others (youth workers, psychologists, philosophers, artists, etc.) had written about similar situations. In my search for simplicity on the other side of complexity, I also tried to understand my sketches as a part of the evolving landscape I was drawing. This was helpful in my efforts to understand and draw the sketches, but I did not make the interpretations part of the sketches unless the characters were actually discussing or interpreting their thoughts, feelings and interactions at the time. As in good literature, I wanted to let their actions, attitudes, and words do the talking.

Using primarily the case analysis skills I developed as a youth worker, I made hundreds of these behind the scene interpretations while I drew my sketches with the wish that I could make them evoke contemplation the way a Hopper painting did (my *Nighthawks*). Some moments defied interpretation. I looked and looked again at these scenes, searching for something, a feeling, or insight, to interpret, and then just settled, knowing there was something that called me to the moment that I knew instinctively made it belong. Because of the unknown, these were the ones I liked the best I think.

Part of my reluctance to interpret, I think, was because of my background. I had sat in many psychoanalytic and psychological case reviews. After a while, many of these began to sound like cliché's. At times, it seemed as if we were trying to apply theory and interpret mostly for ourselves rather than let the kids actions speak for themselves. A disconnect existed between what I saw and what we said. Something just didn't jive. Lack of time and skill, perhaps, kept us from going deeper with our descriptions. I did not want my interpretations to move in that direction, although I knew to some degree they inevitably would.

When I did interpret in my head or on paper as I did in *Basket Hold* I tried to avoid jargon and clichés and focus on the "what *is*" of the moment as poet and philosopher Mark Strand did in this interpretation of a photo from his childhood:

I have a photograph of my mother, my sister, and myself, taken when I was four years old and my mother was thirty-two or so. My sister and I are standing on what must be the front walk to our house then, in front of a hedge, and my mother is crouched in the middle with an arm around each of us. It must be spring because I am wearing shorts and a long sleeved shirt, which is buttoned, probably as a concession to neatness, at the neck. My sister who was then two and a half is wearing a coat that stops just above the knees. The sleeves are too long. It must have been noon or close to it; our common shadow is directly beneath us. My mother's hair is dark and she is smiling. The light spills over her forehead and rides the top or her cheeks, a patch of it rests on the side of her chin. The light falls in the same way on my sister's face and mine. And all our eyes are in the shadow in precisely the same way. I have stared and stared at this photo and each time I have felt a deep and inextricable rush of sadness. Or is it that my mother, who holds both of us, is now dead? Or is it that she is so young, so happy, so proud of her children? Is it the three of us a momentarily bound by the way the light distributes itself in identical ways over each of our faces, binding us together, proclaiming our unity with one another in a past that was just ours and that no one can now share? Or is it simply that we look a bit out of date? Or that whatever we were at the moment catches the heart merely by being over? I suppose all are good reasons for feeling sad and they may account in some part for my feelings, but there is something else I am responding to. It is the presence of the photographer.... (Strand, 2001b, pp 17-18).

In this passage, Strand shows his significant writing and interpreting powers. He sees and looks into the experience. Not only does he show us the photo in context, he interprets and questions it with insight from multiple perspectives. Thus, albeit without Strand's skill or history, this is what I have tried to do in my descriptions and interpretations.

I wrote mostly in the present tense because that's when youth work and my youth occurred—in the present. The present tense also moved the way my reflections and experiences did. Moreover, since self was at the center of the research, I knew the voice had to be mine. Finding my voice, however, was not an easy task. Many fiction writers spend a whole career trying and never find their voice. I searched for mine with the hope that as I got closer to finding it, the reader could relate to my quest to find it. It was a process of writing, rewriting, reading my work (aloud or in my head) over and over until I got the rhythm down and it sounded right, as I tried to do in the fragment of a sketch below.

One on One

> *"30 all," Daniel says.*
> *"32 to 30, my favor," I hunch over with my hands on my knees.*
> *"No. 30 all! Let's go! Take it out!" Daniel snaps a bounce pass to me.*
> *"32, 30," I turn with the ball on my hip and walk to take it out of bounds. Daniel runs behind, bats the ball away, grabs it, charges the basket, takes two steps up the brick wall, leans out in front of the backboard, and dunks the ball. "There now, 32, 32."*
> *I look out the ground level window. It's a cold, grey, fall, Wisconsin day. Leaves have piled up against the grating. We're in the small gym in the basement of the residential center for troubled boys playing one-on-one basketball, or buckets as we call it.*
> *"Let's take a break." I sit down on the scuffed wood floor.*
> *Daniel spins the ball in his hands, stands above me. "What's the matter old man? Ttired?"*
> *"We'll have to rake the leaves later," I say.*

"Not me," Daniel says and changes the topic. "I like this little gym."
"Why?"
"Because I can stuff..."He runs full speed toward the basket and stuffs the ball
again, says, "34,32, my favor...."

In this fragment of a sketch, I tried to make the words move in a way that was consistent with my internal rhythms for hearing and saying them. Youth often referred to this as, "walking the talk." I had to try to show (say) it the way I felt it.

Writing dialogue like finding my voice was difficult. Not only did I have to hear what was said, and how it was said, I had be aware that it was heard with an ear that was used to listening to my voice, or at the very least the rhythms and idiosyncrasies of my voice. The challenge was to capture the gist of what was said, where it was said, in what context it was said, and how it was said. To start, of course, I had to listen and try to develop an ear for dialogue. Whether or not I found mine, I wasn't sure. I was told that I wrote good dialogue, but I didn't have the same confidence. The great writers of dialogue, such as Mamet, Hemingway, and Duras, wrote in a voice that was distinctively theirs. When it came to using dialogue and action to move the story forward they were masters. I read them to see how they did it but I didn't try to copy them. Again, reading my work to my writing teacher seemed to help in this process. While speaking the words aloud in the presence of a listener, I seemed to work harder at trying to hear my inner voice.

By then it was clear that youth work was the work I did with youth as well as the work I did to understand my own youth. To know youth work, I had to know what I brought to the moment so that I could be open and available to mirror back my experience of the other. In a moment of restraint or staring, for instance, such as in the *Basket Hold* sketch, what did I bring and how did that influence what I conveyed to Daniel, as I tried to understand, relate to and connect with him, in a moment of struggle? Similarly, what did I bring to a moment of hesitation, as described in an upcoming sketch that follows titled, *Beach Scene?*

The Existential Hum

This was all easier said than done. Many of the sketches I drew had an element about them I could not understand. There was something I could not quite capture, a stare, a moment of hesitation, an emotion, etc. I referred to this as the existential hum, or "that something" that called to me, a feeling or image that I could not grasp. A rumble I could hear just beneath, or above, my capacity to understand it.

Themes like motion and stillness, for example, always seemed to be trying to say something—something I could hear, but not quite grasp. I had titled my second novel, *In Motion,* because I felt youth work and adolescence was mostly about being in motion--even though I did not completely understand what that meant. Then one day, I came across this passage by former U.S. poet laureate Mark Strand in the introduction to a book of his reflections on Edward Hopper paintings titled simply, *Hopper*:

When I was a child what I saw of the world beyond my immediate neighborhood I saw from the backseat of my parent's car. It was a world glimpsed in passing. It was still. It had its own life and did not know or care that I happened by at that particular time. Like the world of Edward Hopper paintings, it did not return my gaze... These two imperatives—the one that urges us to continue and the one that compels us to stay—create a tension that is constant in Hopper's work (2001a., p.3).

Many of my scenes were like that. I wanted to stay and leave. They presented themselves as if seen from the backseat of my parents' car. I drew and redrew my sketches over and over again until they did not gaze back. It helped remind me that these were experiences I had, not social documents or allegories of unhappiness. This somewhat detached process actually felt more personal. I could see and hear the sketches in the sparse, juxtaposed, clear way they presented themselves to me, and felt "located in the virtual space where the influence and availability of feeling predominated" (Strand, 2001, p. VII).

Philosophers and philosophy also helped me understand phenomena such as motion that seemed to hang at the edge of my consciousness. This passage for instance from the *Essential Foucault* in which the authors spoke about the role of pausing and moving in Michel Foucault's work:

The narrative clarity may well have been a fiction but it was a fiction that helped Foucault to begin working and thinking again. And after his periods of stasis, Foucault usually succeeded in achieving dramatic accelerations in his thinking and action. Thinking was action, and action was motion—and as a thinker and as a person Foucault chose to be in motion... To detach oneself from oneself—such a distance enables motion, and in turn, motion enables a recurrent activity of self detachment. In a certain practice of philosophy, as in science, change, reevaluation, and reformation, is entirely appropriate. For one who searches, such motion lies at the heart of a life devoted to research (In Rabinow and Rose, The Essential Foucault, 1994, p. xxii).

Thus, I was, and remain, curious about how motion, detachment, fiction, research, etc helped me understand self in action (see Chapter 7). I want to know how being in motion, how being still, and how the relationship between the two influenced who I am, was, and how I act now and acted in the past.

Competent Youth Work

Nexus (Krueger, 1995), a book about a day in youth work, was written in part to please a mentor, Henry Maier (1987; 1992; 1995), who challenged me to write a book about competent youth work. I sketched out a day trying to show how central themes from the research and literature in youth work and youth development translated into practice. A few years, ago I taught and consulted at a group home in

Nova Scotia that used the title of this book as its name, and while there witnessed, again to my delight, many of the themes in action.

In the late 1990s, I taught sketching to a group of experienced youth workers, and together we wrote and interpreted their experiences and relationships with youth. This was one of the most significant learning experiences of my career. In our book *Themes and Stories in Youth Work Practice* (Krueger, 2004), we identified themes such as presence, rhythmic interaction, transition, and silence, and practices for increasing understanding and competence among those who worked with our society's most troubled youth (Krueger, Evans, Korsmo, Stanley, and Wilder, 2005). We also investigated youth work as a modern dance in which workers planned their day in advance according to the developmental rhythms of youth then improvised as they moved through the day together (Krueger, 2004).

Part of our motivation was a concern about current trends in the country to define youth as assets, outcomes, and means to the end of a job. In our opinion, youth was being stolen by policymakers, and funding organizations who saw youth mainly as an opportunity to turn teenagers into productive job-holding adults. While this was a good long-term goal, we felt it had been put forward at the expense of accepting youth as a process of human interaction and period of life that was fraught and enriched by all the troubles, downs, ups, insights, experiments, and ecstasies of being human youth. Youth had to *be in* youth before they could be adults, and we wanted to understand more about this part of *being in* youth *with* youth workers.

Juxtaposition, Fragmentation, and Layering

At some point, I'm not sure exactly when, I began to juxtapose, fragment and layer my sketches as Rambo Ronai (1998) did in her study, *Sketching With Derrida: An Ethnography of a Researcher/Erotic Dancer,* in which she used self, and her own playful mix of influences to construct a layered account of striptease dancers, and her ambiguous role. To inform self and the reader, she layered in writing, philosophy, sketching, and systematic sociological introspection.

Similarly, for the reasons explained in a previous section in this chapter, *Vignettes and Postmodernism: The First Sketches,* I experimented with breaking the sketches into smaller fragments, which I juxtaposed with other fragments until I had a sketch comprised of several fragments. Recently I read what Markham (2005) wrote about fragmented narrative and bricolage as interpretive method, but at the time fragmentation simply felt even more consistent with my reflections. Rarely did I see one sketch as a whole. Parts of a sketch (flashes of memory), in combination with parts of other sketches, came at me as I was doing one thing or another. I began to construct new sketches from fragments, mosaics perhaps, such as in the sketch below, which juxtaposes the opening fragment in *Pavilion* with an interaction with Daniel about a year after the *Basket Hold.*

Beach Scene

Daniel pulls on his shorts and leaves the tent. Six other boys from the treatment center are asleep. I wait, and then follow him out of his line of sight. It's a warm August evening in the Door Peninsula, a finger that sticks into Lake Michigan in Wisconsin.

Once he reaches the bluffs, he stands a moment and looks across the water in awe, like perhaps the first Potawatomi to discover the lake's vastness, with the moonlight reflecting off the water across his chest. I duck behind a clump of tall grass and watch as runs down the bluff and glides along the shore on his misty seaside stage. He runs for one hundred yards or so, then he charges up dune and races back down. He repeats these glides and charge until he collapses, exhausted at the water's edge with the small waves washing over him.

Caught up in the mood, I run down the dune hollering at the top of my lungs. Daniel stands and faces me. At the last moment I veer off and dive face first into the water. We splash each other and sit on the beach with our chins on our knees.

"Do you think I'll be fucked up like my ol' man?" Daniel asks, his voice shivering.

I hesitate, say, "No."

*

(years earlier) I can hear them talking.
"How did you feel when Father died?" my uncle asks my father.
"Like the boy in James Joyce's story about the dead priest, sad and relieved."
"It was different when Mother died, wasn't it?" my uncle asks.
"Yes, God forgive us if we ever lose the benignity she tried to instill in us," my father says.
"Yes, God forgive them, Verona," my mother sighs to my aunt.

They, my aunt, uncle, father, and mother, are in the kitchen of our second story flat on Milwaukee's Northwest Side, drinking cocktails. I'm in my bedroom—fourteen going on fifteen. It's about 11:00 PM. My older brother is asleep in his bed across the room.

After the company is gone, and the house is dark, I get dressed and go into the kitchen. Something moves. My father is dancing in the moonlight in the living room. Hidden from view, I watch as he moves in and out of the shadows from the elm branches that cathedral the narrow street in front of the house. He's wearing the shirt and tie he wore to the life insurance company he's worked at all his adult life. With his hands in his pockets and his pant legs raised, he shuffles his feet to the music in his head. When he turns toward the window, the moon shines on his face. He's smiling, but his eyes seem far away.

*

"I do not know what the spirit of a philosopher could more wish to be than a good dancer. For the dance is his ideal, also his art, finally also the only kind of piety he knows, his divine spirit," I remember a quote I cannot find from Nietzsche and use it in the adolescent development class I teach to describe the importance of presence, history, culture, and rhythm in interactions with youth.

Daniel and I had been through hell together. More than once he had run away. He had tried to hit me several times. He had spit at me and said some things I would not repeat. Yet we had endured and our relationship had grown stronger. At this point I trusted him and myself in this moment. I let him go that night whereas in the past I would have made an effort to stop him. I was curious about where he was going. I watched in admiration of how he unleashed his raw energy. It was almost as if he had created a stage to temporarily exorcise the demons that haunted him. An act of great beauty and sadness, the lead actor collapsed at the water's edge. This was not familiar turf for him. He had not been out of the city. His world, like many of our youth, was limited to the hood, the center of the city, and that was it. For some reason, he disclosed how he was feeling in that moment, something that he had not done before.

I wanted to be part of the drama, to place myself in it with the same intensity, to scream at the top of my lungs. I did it. We played and splashed together revealing something more in both of us, a desire to express, to be what we did together. He was there and I was there in the moment.

Then, as we sat together in one of those unforgettable moments with the moon running across the water to our feet, he shared for the first time his fear that he would end up like the father that had so terribly abused him an his sister. I hesitated before I said no.

Why did I hesitate? Did I know on some level that I did not need to make things better, yet tried anyway? Did the mood of the moment make it impossible to resist even though I knew deep down that it might not be? Was I assuring myself, once again, that I would not end up like my father, a company man? Was I anxious and uncertain, like him, not just shivering from the cold?

There was and is still something from this moment that haunts me, something more to be learned. Even though my response was not the response I would give today, it was a moment of human connection, I'm sure of that, but I'm not sure exactly why. The conditions were perfect. It was just he and I alone on the beach, vulnerable, open to discovering something about us. He must have known, like I did, that there were no guarantees about the future, and that my hesitation reflected my true feelings. He probably wanted the assurance anyway. But I'm still not sure that that's the whole story.

Finally, the Nietzsche quote seemed to fit. There was something about rhythm, the dance, etc. in both fragments. Thinking of Nietzsche, and then philosophers like Foucault who wrote about the care of self as the ethos of civilized societies brought to the sketch another and perhaps deeper element of interpretation. In *Themes and Stories,* we wrote about the importance of being light on our feet, of bringing ourselves to the moment with self-awareness and curiosity at the edge of our consciousness, in a way that freed us to be in the dance.

Montage

My fondness for movies and the many parallels with qualitative inquiry and film influenced the way I sketched. In their introduction to Handbook of Qualitative Research, Denzin and Lincoln (2004) wrote, "Montage uses brief images to create a clearly defined sense of urgency and complexity. Montage invites viewers to construct interpretations that build on one another as the scene unfolds (p. 5)."

I liked the idea of a scene unfolding in juxtaposed, moving images. In a book of interviews with the author titled, On Film, German filmmaker Wim Wenders (2001, pp. 326-327) spoke about how good montage is like a great sum of images that is only as good as the trueness of each image. Further, similar to Strand (2001) in his interpretation of Hopper paintings, Wenders spoke about the truthfulness of images when seen through the eyes of eyes of a child. He also spoke about the importance of continuity of movement, which can be witnessed in films like Paris Texas and Wings of Desires where the trueness of the image and continuity of movement take the viewer into the life of the character with the sense that something is going on that is worthy of discovering, something related to self.

Sam Shepard, who worked with Wenders on *Paris Texas,* did this beautifully in plays like *Fool for Love,* which was also made into a movie. Recently I saw a documentary of Bob Dylan, *No Direction Home,* by Martin Scorcese. He started in 1966 and kept moving back and forth to pivotal moments in that showed meaning that might not have been achieved in any other form. Similarly, in documentaries related to youth work like *Dog Town and the Z Boys,* and films like, *Raising Victor Vargas,* I saw lives in fragments and forms that opened me to new interpretations.

In most, if not all good films there was also a scaffolding toward some key idea or theme or understanding. The work builds toward something. It might take a twist but always comes and moves back to a place that moves it toward something that is inextricably central to what the film is about, a feeling, mood, person, political cause, or a becoming as Che' Guevara became in *Motorcycle Diaries.*

Like many other film buffs, sometimes I feel like I missed my calling and should have been a filmmaker. Perhaps this is part of the reason why sketching draws on film in an attempt to combine and move images in a way that tells the story and presents the "data" in a way that leads to new discoveries. In this context, the movement of the characters and their words and the spaces in between the words deserve attention.

Thematic Analysis

Literature, film, qualitative inquiry, and a number of disciplines and genres taught me about different ways to conduct thematic analysis. All in some manner require delving into the material to look for patterns or threads that run through a story, painting, film, etc. The examiner looks at and/or reads and rereads the material over and over again until it is apparent that a theme central to the work becomes apparent.

In sketching I discovered themes much the way I interpreted. I looked at several sketches instead of one sketch, searching for patterns, as I fragmented and juxtaposed on paper and in my mind. It was like looking through a kaleidoscope. I twisted and turned the images in my mind until patterns emerge then went back to look in more detail to see if these were indeed key themes. Sometimes I used a theme or found a new emphasis for a theme as I drew a new sketch. I was never quite sure how this worked. In other words, I didn't know if a theme spurred on a sketch or if it surfaced from a sketch or both. Death, identity, loss, connection were a few themes that ran through my narratives as they run through many narratives. My themes were not new. Others had experienced and written about them at length, but not from my perspective.

Experimental Autobiography

After reading and discussing the work of Cezanne with Suzanne and her friend another artist, I began to think of my sketches as brushstrokes on my landscape that I left behind as I reached out for an image. Together they created some kind of abstraction, a self portrait perhaps. Then one day, after I had drawn and juxtaposed dozens of more sketches, many of which were based on my life outside youth work, I read this passage in the preface to *Philosophical Investigations:*

> "The same or almost the same points were always being approached afresh from different directions and new sketches made. Very many of these were badly drawn or uncharacteristic, marked by all the defects of a weak draftsman. And when they were rejected a number of tolerable ones were left, which now had to be rearranged and cut down, so that if you looked at them you could get a picture of a landscape. Thus the book is really only an album" *(Wittgenstein, 2001, pages* unnumbered).

Although written in a different context, this reinforced what I had been thinking: if I could find a way to organize and cut down the sketches, I might be able to draw a discernable, if imperfect, personal landscape or self-portrait. So with Schopenhauer's notion of man as the sum of his experiences, and books like *A Portrait of the Artist as Young Man* in mind, I began to draw a self-portrait (Ellis and Bochner, 2000; Fewster, 1999). Maybe this was what I had been doing all along—looking for the experiences that came to bare in a moment of hesitation, or a stare, and how it influenced me as part of those and similar moments when I tried to learn, connect, discover, and empower youth. If I was open, and available, to mirror back my experiences of youth as we played and interacted and talked, what had made me the way I was in those moments?

Perhaps I was also trying to use sketching as another means to help me as Foucault (Rabinow and Rose, 1994, pp 25-42) argued find "care for self" as an ethos for caring for kids. I had known for years that in order to care for others we had to care for self, but had I really done that in the context of knowing and valuing my own experience?

Mostly, however, I was fascinated about what I had written at the end of my book *Nexus,* when I called youth work a process of self in action in which workers and youth moved in and out of synch with each others rhythms for trusting and growing. I wanted to know the self that I brought to action, or the self awareness that was at the edge of my consciousness when I interacted with youth, my own and others. Not the self that consumed me, but the self that made me in the moment, the self that was present and brought with it all that had proceeded to make me a youth worker at that particular moment in time. Sketching, in this regard, was and is, the homework I do so that I can be free in the moments of hesitation, stillness, motion, conflict, etc., with youth to understand what *is.*

I thought it would be interesting to see how some of the most important sketches in my life looked together. So I explored many combinations. There was no particular order for doing this. Sometimes I put sketches together by feel and other times I put them together by association. I also tried to follow, whenever I could, the spontaneous way in which they appeared in reflection.

One of the new drawings became a play because that seemed to be the best way to frame and move the dialogue. Several fragments worked best alone and were turned into poems. Many sketches and fragments were dropped. These were either still badly drawn, or simply didn't fit. Gradually, a central narrative emerged from the moments that I returned to with curiosity and fondness over and over again. Many of the experiences I wrote about were from my own youth. This reminded me that a large portion of youth work was the work I did to understand this period of my life. It also provided different twists on themes, such as presence, transitions, identity, death, and repetition, that were identified in my study with youth workers as part of youth work, youth, and life. Seven sketches, each constructed from several fragments, and an epilogue remained. I titled the entire collection, *Pavilion: A Portrait of a Youth Worker* (Krueger, 2006b). *Pavilion* was chosen as the title because a park pavilion was a place I often went to as a youth and ran past on my daily run as an adult, and because it meant temporary shelter, and the inner ear, which I thought was appropriate in relationship to my search for place, as in place the is one's self, and to hear my experience as deeply as I could.

I saw my work in this regard as my version of *testimonio.* I was researcher/author of my story, and by trying to tell it, and show it, in my historical and cultural context, I hoped it would lead to social change and truth, which I believed was crucial to the wellbeing of youth (Teirney, 2000, p. 539-541). An activist in a struggle that had not been resolved, I was continuing the discourse by attempting to define my life in its history and culture, thus shedding new light on youth, and/or how understanding our own youth influences our ability to understand the other, often more troubled youth. More than anything else youth called for understanding and I was contributing what I could to this quest.

Whether or not this is best categorized as experimental, fictional, autobiography or memoir I am not sure (Bikerts, 2006). *Pavilion* is a collection of sketches, fragments, etc. that appear at a certain point in time instrumental in creating my self portrait, or collage of experiences. Further, while based on my experiences over sixty years, these are not, as playwright Sam Shepard said in a documentary about the making of his play based on his relationship with his father, "xerox copies" (Almereyda, 2001).

There are many more technological, methodological, moral, philosophical, and personal arguments that supported my points of view and methods. I will assume the reader can make some of these associations. I am always conflicted about explaining my work. Like most creative writers, I want my work to stand for itself. At the same time, I enjoy reading about other authors' histories, processes, and influences. It helps in many cases, I find, to know a little about the author, and/or the subjects beforehand.

SUMMARY

When I started to draw sketches, I was shifting my attention from the technique, method, data, outcomes and facts of youth work, to the experience of youth work and what it was as I read about it and recalled my experiences. This was not an attempt to minimize the importance of these other ways of looking at the work, but rather to try to hear and understand what youth work *is* in my lived experience. After years of experience, I had come to the conclusion, like many others, that in order to truly know and be effective at youth work I had to be willing to dig into my experiences and life (go deeper), and look to the questions and pearls that these experiences offered. And in doing this, as a member of the effort to build the field of youth work I tried to make myself visible (Hans Skott-Myhre, p. 221) in a way that showed I valued the *other*.

I also wanted to focus on youth work as a "process" of human interaction. The movement toward outcomes, evidence-based and best practices, and other end points in youth work, as in other fields, seemed to be undermining and distracting people, including myself, from thinking about what *is,* and was, going on in daily interactions. Moreover, most of the studies, which were hastily designed to prove the results needed to justify the funding, seemed to break down because significant links could not be made between what actually existed and was being done and the result. The numbers did not connect to the relationships between worker, self, and youth. Mainly because no one took time to describe how people got to the end points.

Philosopher Jacob Needleman has written and spoken about how important it is for people to stop and think without any intended outcome other than to really explore a subject in depth (see www.jacobneedleman.com). Better action will follow, he argues, if we do this. Czech novelist Milan Kundera summed this up for me in an interview when he said, "The novelist teaches the reader to comprehend the world as a question. There is wisdom and tolerance in that approach...In any case it seems to me that people all over the world today prefer to judge rather than understand, to answer rather than ask, so that the voice of the novel can barely be heard above the foolishness of human certainties (In 2001 Roth, p. 100)."

I sketched to question, understand, and show self in action as an ever-changing phenomenon, to know by digging deeper with wisdom and tolerance into the experiences I brought to my work. In closing, while writing this chapter I heard the following Leonard Cohen song, a poem set to music, which seemed appropriate:

Villanelle for Our Time

From bitter searching of the heart,
Quickened with passion and with pain
We rise to play a greater part.
This is the faith from which we start:
Men shall know commonwealth again
From bitter searching of the heart.

We loved the easy and the smart,
But now with keener hand and brain,
We rise to play a greater part,
The lesser loyalties depart,
And neither race nor creed remain

From bitter searching of the heart.
Not steering by the venal chart
That tricked the mass for private gain,
We rise to play a greater part.
Reshaping narrow law and art...

Leonard Cohen song, Villanelle for Our Time--words written by Frank Scott (1899-1985) found in the insert to the Lenard Cohen Dear Heather CD.

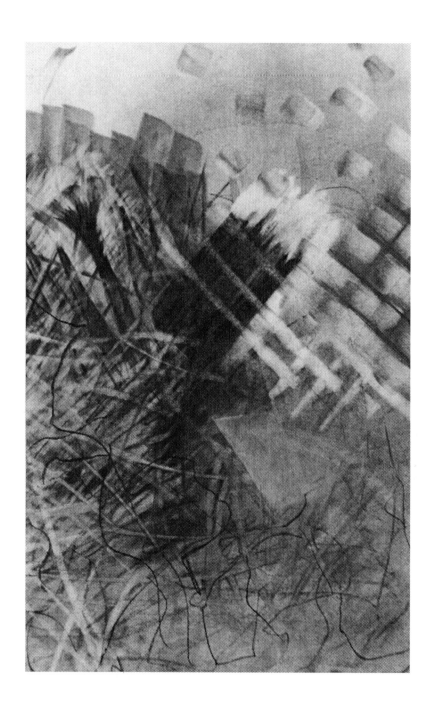

YOUTH WORK *IS*

Nicole and Matt are working with six youth: Cathie, Maria, Ramon, Ron, Cheryl, and Nick at the group home, Nexus, a two-story house in the center of a medium-sized city. It's an older building that has been decorated and livened with the youths' art and music.

Nicole is sitting with Cathie, Maria and Ramon at the dining room table, working on budgets. She is teaching them how to manage money, a skill they will need when they leave the group home and have to live on their own.

"My parents never had a budget," Maria says.

"Neither did mine. They never sat down like this and wrote down how they would spend their money," Ramon says.

"Each family does it a little differently. My parents didn't do it quite like this, but I find it helpful myself to have a budget, otherwise I tend to spend more than I have," Nicole says.

"How can you spend more than you have?" Cathie asks.

"Charge cards."

"Yeah, I can't wait to get a charge card," Ramon says.

"Charge cards can be helpful, especially if you don't want to carry a lot of money, but they can also be a problem."

"How?" Maria asks.

"You spend more than you can pay back and get further and further in debt," Nicole says.

"We're leaving now," Matt, Nicole's co-worker says, as he walks through the dining room with three other youth: Nick, Cheryl, and Ron. They are on their way to the playground to play basketball. It's a familiar walk, one they take together two or three times a week together.

Nick is sad and worried. He's leaving the group home. In a few days he'll be going into independent living. Like the other youth in the program, at age 18, he will have to make in it on his own...

As I mentioned in Chapter 2, a mentor, Henry Maier (1987, 1992; 1995), challenged me to write a book about competent youth work. In part to please him, I decided to take a stab at it, and the result was *Nexus: A Book about Youth Work* that described a day in youth work at a multifaceted agency for youth. The above sketch is an example of how I constructed the book from several sketches that were based on my experiences, the experiences of youth workers I had worked and studied with, and two reviews of the research and literature in the field (Krueger, 1991a, 1991b).

In the years that followed publication of the book, I continued to write a column by the same title for the *Journal of Child and Youth Care Work* in which I tried to show how some of the latest theory and research in the field translated into practice. *Nexus* was chosen as the title of the book, the name of the group home, and the title of the column, to represent the many interconnected themes and practices from the research and writing in the field that were woven into and through youth work practice by youth workers and youth. A "spaghetti bowl" of ideas, concepts, values and practices, as a colleague called it.

In writing about Nexus, which I see as an ongoing process, I am trying to define what youth work *is,* as I interpret it, at a certain moment in time. If I were to define youth work in general today, my definition would include the following:

A PROCESS OF HUMAN INTERACTION

Youth work, in the brief example above, is portrayed as an interpersonal (*among human beings*), inter-subjective (*with different viewpoints and feelings*), contextual (*each person, situation and environment unique*) process that occurs in the lived experience, or as it is sometimes referred to as "the daily living environment," "the community," or "the streets." Further, as a process of human interaction, youth work is enriched and fraught with all the emotions, challenges, struggles and discoveries that are part of being human. Workers try their best and learn from their successes and failures.

Central to this process is self. Workers bring self to the moment and learn from their feelings and insights as they interact with and learn from youth. Workers do their homework, as I tried to do in the previous chapter, so they can understand how their histories bias and influence their interactions. They also try to be aware of their feelings of fear, anger, joy, excitement, boredom, sadness etc. as they interact. Youth work, in this context, is a process of self in action. Workers use self to inform and be in their interactions.

There are many underlying theories and practices that apply to youth work as an interactive process. In general, for the purpose of discussion here, these fall into two categories, developmental care and postmodern, story/narrative based.

Developmental Care theories and associated practices suggest youth and youth workers are developing beings, each at a unique place or phase in his or her social, emotional, cognitive, and physical development (Maier, 1987; 1995, VanderVen, 1999a). From this perspective, the goal is to be *in* development *with* youth and to constantly seek ways to learn and grow while experiencing the moment and/or activity together. Youth work, in this regard, is primarily a process of weaving as much care, learning, and counseling as possible into daily interactions with the awareness of the cognitive, social, emotional, and physical developmental needs and strengths of each youth. Obviously, this is a complex and daunting task that requires knowledge of the research and theory and practices in adolescent development. Suffice it to say for now that, competent youth work, as in any human service work, requires considerable study and practice.

Again, for the sake of simplicity, I believe an argument can be made that the goal is to create as many moments of connection, discovery, and empowerment as possible because these moments change youth's stories and fuel their development (Garfat, 1998; Krueger, 2004; Maier, 1987; 1995). Briefly, a moment of connection occurs when a worker and a youth feel they are experiencing a moment or activity together. A moment of discovery occurs when a youth has an insight, solves a problem or figures something out about his or her self, and/or the world around him or her. A moment of empowerment occurs when a youth feels like he or she can do or try something even if they could fail.

These moments nourish development and become part of their evolving narratives. Youth who experience their fair share of these moments, in other words, are likely to develop skills and have stories that will help them take on the challenges of daily living, and have fulfilling lives.

Postmodern: Story Based theories and practices suggest that youth and workers build and shape themselves into the world through unique cultural, communal and familial experiences, and subsequently the way they make meaning depends on the stories (evolving narratives) they bring to their experiences and interactions (Bruner, 1990). This might cautiously be called a postmodern view. In defining postmodernism as it relates to child and youth care Karen Vander Ven (1999b) wrote:

> ....postmodernism emerged in the face of disillusionment with modernity which contends that there is a complete truth that can be sought by methodologically rational scientific inquiry....In postmodern thought, however, knowledge is considered to be socially constructed by individuals in their interactions with others, and is shaped by the context in which they live. Meaning is conferred to any situation by the perspectives people bring to it from their own subjective value systems (p. 294).

This definition captures how youth workers view life as a process of human interaction in which "meaning is conferred to any situation by the perspectives people bring to it from their own subjective value systems (cultures, families, communities, etc.)" New meanings are made each time a person interacts with another person in a specific context or situation and these meanings become part of their evolving narratives.

Nicole, for example, has a discussion with the youth about budgets with sensitivity to the different meanings these discussions have for the youth and their families. In another situation a worker might take a group of youth from the residential treatment center camping. One night the worker sits with a youth around a campfire talking about the youth's family. It's the first time the youth has been out of the city. The worker has been camping many times. The youth's meaning of family is different than the workers meaning of family. The youth's parents were abusive, whereas the worker came from a caring family. As they talk the worker asks, "What was it like for you?" trying to understand. Their conversation is

41

influenced by the surroundings (fire, woods, stars, etc.), their words, and the connection they feel with each other. Afterwards, the meaning of family, camping, campfires, and human connection has changed slightly for both of them.

Thus, from this perspective, no two youth or workers at Nexus, or anywhere, have the same narratives, or experiences and all interactions are unique and occur in unique contexts. An experience we have is ours and ours alone. It will not occur in the same way again. The meaning has changed with time as we reflect back on it with hindsight. A person who reads it will make his or her own meaning of it based on his or her experience, and so forth.

Two Competencies: Empathy and Listening

Recently, several hundred practitioners, educators, and researchers from across North America identified and described numerous knowledge areas and competencies (Mattingly, 2004) for effective youth work practice. One of the most important competencies and attributes for our discussion here is *empathy*: the ability to be aware of your experiences in a way that makes you curious about, value and want to understand the experiences of others. Workers with empathy, for example, do not project their experiences on to youth or project themselves into the youth's experiences. They try to understand how a youth is feeling about or seeing a situation while negotiating and being aware of the role of power, authority, gender, race, etc. in their interactions and transactions.

When I talk about empathy in my youth work classes I usually say something like, "It isn't about putting yourself in someone else's shoes because you never can. It's about being curious and wanting to understand the other person's story. If we value our own unique experiences, then this should open us to being curious about and valuing the experience of the other. We can never have the experience of another person. We can only have our experience that in turn can be used to try to understand the experience of another person."

Interconnected with empathy is *listening*, or the ability hear what youth say. More than anything else, perhaps, youth want to be heard. Not just listened to, but heard and understood. In class I often say "There is nothing more powerful that we can do than give youth our undivided attention and try to understand. To be there fully for youth with an interest and concern about what they say. This is very hard to do, especially when there are many youth trying to be heard at the same time, or if we are tired or distracted.

These two competencies along with the competencies and themes discussed later are central, I believe, to creating moments of connection, discovery, and empowerment and making meaning with youth. Mastering them, like many aspects of youth work, is a career long goal.

The shift at Nexus continues at the basketball court:

It's a warm fall day. They choose sides. Cheryl and Ron will play Nick and Matt. As they warm up with jumpers and hook shots, they playfully try to block each other's shots.

The early moments of the game go smoothly, as if choreographed by their history of playing together. They know and anticipate each other's moves. The score bounces back and forth. A shot is blocked, a rebound grabbed, a ball falls cleanly through the net.

During the game, similar to the way he works with them in other activities, Matt tries to get a feel for where each youth is and positions himself in a way that he can help advance the game. After about forty-five minutes of play, the score is tied. They take a break and drink from the jar of ice water Matt brought from the group home. Nick sits next to Matt on the asphalt with his back to the chain link fence. As Cheryl and Ron stand nearby, ribbing rib one another about an errant pass or blocked shot, Nick begins to think again about his departure from the group home. Then he stands and knocks the ball out of Ron's hands and the game is on again.

The pace intensifies. Matt and Nick stretch the lead, then the others catch up and go ahead. Nick shoves Ron as he goes for a loose ball. Ron turns and gets in Nick's face. "Cool it," Matt says, holding the ball. He waits until they back away from each other and throws the ball back into play.

Cheryl scores, putting her team ahead by four. On the inbounds, Matt passes to Nick in the corner. He goes up for a jumper. Ron times his leap perfectly and blocks the ball an instant after it leaves Nick's hand.

"Foul!" Nick shouts.

"Bull, it was clean," Ron responds, mocking Nick by imitating how he blocked the shot.

"Fuck you!"

Fists clenched by his side, Ron walks slowly toward Nick.

Matt steps in between them.

"He's just worried about leaving," Ron says.

"No I'm not, motha fucker," Nick responds.

Ron raises his fists, lunges forward, pretending he's ready to fight.

"Cool it, Ron! You too, Nick. Let's take a break," Matt says.

"I don't need to settle down. He fouled me," Nick points at Ron.

"Ron and Cheryl, take a few shots at the other end while I talk to Nick," Matt says and motions for Nick to follow him to the side of the court.

"Why do I have to talk to you? He's the one who started it."

Matt takes a drink of ice water and hands it to Nick, then says, "Look, I understand about your leaving. I'm going to miss you and so are the rest of the guys, but getting into it with Ron won't help. If you want to talk, I'm here to listen."

"I don't want to talk about it here."

"Okay, later then, but cool it for the rest of the game."

Nick looks down at his shoes.

"Nick," Matt says, waiting for a response.
Nick nods, reluctantly.
"Okay, let's get rolling," Matt shouts and the game regains its earlier rhythm.
They play for about fifteen more minutes. Cheryl and Ron win by a basket.
"Good game," Matt says, then looks at Nick and playfully bumps him on the shoulder.
"Yeah, good game," Nick says.

In this and the preceding excerpt from a shift at Nexus, Matt tries to connect, problem solve, and create opportunities for youth to feel empowered. He interacts with an awareness of the developmental needs and strengths of the youth and the stories they bring to the interaction. If we examine, for example, these last few interactions in the context of what preceded it with an awareness of Nick's feeling about his upcoming home visit, any number of factors can be questioned and discussed related to theories of human and relationship development, and the stories that the youth bring and make as they interact, including themes such as boundaries, self disclosure, tempo, rhythmic interaction, timing, position, proximity, etc., which I will discuss or show in more detail later, and are central to the translation of these theories into practice.

Themes

In general, a theme is a phenomenon (competency, action, feeling, attitude, etc.) that permeates interactions in youth work and is interconnected with other important themes that are part of the ever changing nexus (spaghetti bowl) of themes that define youth work or field at a certain point in time. At the end of the *Nexus* book, I identified several themes in youth work. In the study I did with youth workers we identified twenty-five themes that were central to their sketches (Krueger, 2004). To identify these themes, each of us wrote, read out loud and interpreted sketches we had written (our own and others). As we read and critiqued the sketches, we also searched for themes in the interactions portrayed in the sketches. Many of the themes we identified had been identified previously by other researchers (Garfat, 1998; Krueger, 1991; 1995, 2004; Nakulla and Ravitch, 1998), such as *listening, empathy, being in the moment, body language, touch, boundaries, cross cultural communication, conflict resolution* and *being dependable*. We tried to add insight to the discussion about these themes as we showed them in our sketches. New themes that had not received much attention such as silence also moved to the forefront in our discussion. Many of these themes are apparent in the previous and following sections of the *Nexus* sketch, which was constructed in part with the themes in mind:

The smell of tacos has filled the group home, a duplex that was converted a few years ago into a group home for youth transitioning to independent living. It's full of symbols of youth—posters, pictures, music and magazines that say this is a place where young people live and this is who they are.

Cathie, Maria, and Ramon are in the kitchen helping Nicole maker dinner. This is one of many activities they engage in to develop the skills and feelings they will need when they live on their own. Throughout the day they do chores and develop skills that will help them when they get full time jobs. They also learn how to problem solve, open banking accounts, drive a car and talk about their feelings.

Maria and Nicole are chopping lettuce, tomatoes, onions and green peppers for the tacos. Ramon is grating cheese. Cathie is frying ground beef.

"When will we eat, I'm starving?" Ron asks.

"In a few minutes; you can set the table," Nicole responds.

Nick, Matt, and Cheryl help Ron set the table while Nicole and the other boys put the food into bowls and set it in the middle of the table. Before they sit down, Matt lowers the volume of the music. Each meal begins by having one youth share something that happened during their day. Tonight it's Cheryl's turn. "Ron and I crushed Nick and Matt in two-on-two," she says, imitating a jumper by flicking her wrist in front of her face.

"Crushed us? What game were you playing in," Matt jokes.

"Two f...lousy points," Nick says, catching himself before he says the curse word.

"Pass the cheese, I'm starving," Ron says, preparing his taco. The bowls begin to move around the table, passed from one hand to another as the girls, boys and workers build tacos.

As the conversation and the meal take on a rhythm of their own, there is a sense of harmony, but then suddenly the rhythm is interrupted. "Give me that!" Ramon shouts at Maria.

Nicole looks at Ramon.

"She's hogging the tomatoes," Ramon says.

"Maria, pass Ramon the tomatoes," Nicole says.

The meal regains its flow. After dessert, they work together to clean up. There is some jostling, swearing and playful teasing as they wash and dry the dishes together. Matt and Nicole treat each situation in context, ignoring some incidents and intervening in others, then the youth go to their rooms to study.

If we were to break this section, and the previous sections of the Nexus sketch down, or "deconstruct it," we could discuss and question it in relationship to many of the themes presented earlier. Rhythmic interaction (Maier, 1992), proximity (Redl and Wineman, 1957), cross cultural communication, and conflict resolution (Powell, 1990) at one point or another permeate the interactions with the youth at dinner. Further interpretation is left up to you for now. The point here is that themes like these, along with many of the competencies and techniques that have been identified as central to effective practice, can inform the way youth work is practiced.

Following are a few themes that I am curious about today. These are themes that often appear in moments of connection, discovery and empowerment in the stories of youth workers about their interactions with youth:

A way of being in which the verbs and prepositions—act, do, in, with, etc.-- move to the forefront of the language and action. As workers and youth make dinner, for example, they are *in* the moment *with* each other experiencing life, learning and growing together, each one getting something from the journey as the other as they *interact, act, and/or do.* You/I/ we, together in this situation, for our own, and each other's, benefits, for all its worth: the paradoxes, contradictions, struggles, insights, sadness, joy, failure and success.

Curiosity, wanting to know what it's like for self and the other, nothing taken for granted, always the possibility for new insight and meaning, a chance to connect, discover, and empower through being with, and curious, about one another and the surroundings.

The here and now--the moments in which youth and workers biographies and histories give way to the present (Baizerman, 1992). Workers and youth doing, acting and interacting with the intent and purpose of being *in* youth, an end in and of itself rather than a means to an end, time embodied in actions, interactions, and motions. A worker and group of youths working on a clean-up project immersed in the moment and their work, the process as important as completing the job, the goal of being with one another as important as the goal to clean the room.

Presence, workers in the moment, open and available to mirror back their experience of youth--eyes focused and attentive, listening with undivided attention, curious, enthusiastic, serious, sad, happy or whatever emotion the other and/or the situation evokes (Fewster, 1999). Workers "walking the talk" and "being real," conveying the message I am here, aware, and ready to go with you," as youth learn presence from and with workers. A way of being, eyes fixed on specific points, and a sense of comfort with the space that is oneself (Ortiz, 1992, p. 128).

Development in action, or development as it is known and experienced in the moment, the focus on what is done in relationship to, how the youth and the workers develop in their interactions, actions, and non-actions (Maier, 1987; Vander Ven, 1999). A sense of what development is as perceived and experienced by the participants and how this fits or does not fit with our intent--to be in development with youth.

Care as a feeling and action (Austin and Halpin, 1990). Care work, walking the talk--cleaning the floor, wiping noses, feeding, being there, and pitching in, unconditionally and nonjudgmentally--workers caring for all the kids, not liking all of them all the time, but always acting with care with them all.

Care of Self as "Ethos" (Foucault in Rabinow and Rose 2003, p. 25-42), workers and organizations caring for self so they can care for others--a worker's pain or anger understood and cared for so he or she can care for an angry youth or youth in pain, a worker's well being central to creating an environment that nurtures and promotes a youth's wellbeing. Workers and organizations valuing self and freedom, not imposing self on or attempting to control the other, and seeking opportunities for the other to be empowered. (In this regard, empowerment is not given, one does not empower someone else but rather the other feels empowered while doing something and being with the other.)

Rhythmic Interaction, workers and youth moving in and out of synch with each other's rhythms for trusting and growing. Workers and youth playing catch in harmony, the tossing of the ball forming a natural connection, or sensing they are out of synch," and searching for a shared rhythm. Intentionally changing to a pleasing, safe rhythm to move the action forward or overcome boredom (Maier, 1992). A worker is out of synch. He searches for resolution, knowing that it is this process of being in and out of synch that leads to connection, discovery, and empowerment.

Seeking Resolution, as workers and youth try to connect, discover, and empower. Workers and youth struggling, scrapping, and challenging one another. One moment leading to another in the dance of child and youth care: struggle and resolution, failure and success, sadness and joy, interconnected. A worker restrains a youth until slowly they both feel safe again; after a short time-out a youth is ready to reengage. A youth uses foul language to express her anger. The worker reframes the situation and they speak about their different perceptions of the event until a common ground is found or they let go of the issue and move on.

Unordinary, nothing is ordinary, every moment different, the circumstances from which youth and workers come from make it impossible to generalize or assume that someone knows or has experienced something. Many of the youth have experienced relationships and interactions that fall outside what society might assume are the norms (Ward, 2004) . Having a meal around a dinner table might be a totally new experience, being touched might have a different meaning than the one intended, or a bed in a single room might be unfamiliar. Even a common, ordinary, everyday, experience such as getting dressed might be perceived differently by each participant.

Speaking across the spaces of experiences: workers and youth learning from and about each other, and how their culture influences each of them as they speak to one another—multicultural youth work as in a conversation: This is what it is like for me, what is it like for you? (a.k.a. meaning making) while seeking common ground or a place of mutual reality, or doing something, an activity or chore, in a way that makes new meaning, or something more meaningful.

Space and place as in the space and place that is one's self. The space that shapes us, or the place we long for. Being in these spaces and places, with others and alone, using space and place to promote development, relocating or being in a place because is a good place to "hang out," play ball, be quiet, dream, just be, or be sad.

Work, hard, good, gut wrenching, energetic work--workers rolling up their sleeves and getting into the thick of it, then going home tired, and sometimes exhausted. No "ifs, ands, or buts," about it. You've got to want to be in it, and in physical and emotional condition to do it!

Questioning, asking what does it look like from this perspective or that perspective? If I did this, then what would happen? If I did that, what would happen? How could I have done it differently? Is it possible the youth saw the situation differently? This is what it's like for me; I wonder how it is for him or her? How would this philosopher or that practitioner have interpreted the situation? Could it possibly mean this?

Shift at Nexus continues:

During study hour, Matt and Nicole make sure that each youth gets individual attention. The tone of the group home is compatible with study, with both quiet background music and noise, as they question and praise the youth, looking for moments of connection and discovery. "How do you think that problem might be solved?" Matt asks. He stands behind Maria, who is at the desk in her room, and puts his hand on her shoulder.

"What's another way of thinking about what that story means?" Nicole asks Ron as she sits with him in the living room reading a short story for his literature class.

After study hour they break into two groups. Cathie, Maria, and Ron go with Matt to watch a documentary on jazz and the other three go with Nicole to the recreation room in the basement to continue work on a mural. The mural is a work in progress that covers and circles the walls in the recreation room. Each youth is asked to add something that is an expression of him-or her. What they paint is entirely up to them as long as they do it with respect for the work of the others and the spirit of the mural. No gang symbols, swearing, or scenes of graphic sex or violence. They work together, each youth and Nicole, in his or her own space.

"I like that, especially the color scheme," Nicole says to Cheryl.

"It's a mandala. We were learning about them in class," Cheryl explains to Nicole.

Upstairs the others are watching the documentary about the history of jazz and blues and its many leaders.

"I told you the brothers started rock and roll. Jazz, blues, and then rock and roll. Elvis, this guy Benny Goodman, they were just along for the ride," Ron says.

"Yeah, but they got all the money," Cathie says.

"I never knew all this," Maria says.

"Man, where you been?" Ron replies.

Matt comes in with a bowl of popcorn, hands each boy a napkin and soft drink. He's learning as much about music as the boys are.

"Hip hop comes from jazz," Ron says. "It all does."

Nicole pokes her head in the room. "I thought I smelled popcorn. I'll get the others and we'll join you.

"Good," Matt says.

Ron and Nick quickly fill their napkins with popcorn.

"I can make more, don't worry, there'll be plenty," Matt says.

The youth and workers sit together on the floor in harmony, eating popcorn and watching the rest of the documentary. Then it's time for bed. Nicole turns off the TV and picks up the empty bowl of popcorn. Matt turns on some quiet music and says, "Okay, let's go."

There is some playful pushing and shoving as the boys climb the stairs and take turns using the bathroom. Matt and Nicole help them straighten their things and get their materials ready for school.

"Lights out," Nicole says.

Each youth slowly gets into bed. Ron and Ramon, roommates, like a little quiet music as they fall to sleep. Cheryl likes her room totally dark. Cathie and Maria leave the blinds open so the streetlight can shine through. Nick, like most of the youth when they are getting near the time to leave, has his own room.

Nicole and Matt spend a little time with each boy, giving them the attention they need. Some youth like to talk a little, others just need a friendly goodnight and perhaps a hand on the shoulder or cover pulled up to their chin. Nicole stops in Nick's room last. He's still reading.

"C'mon, time for lights out," Nicole says.

"I know, I was just reading a little longer. This book is hard to read, but it's really good," Nick says referring to A Portrait of The Artist as a Young Man.

"Yes, it was hard for me too," Nicole says.

"The author is really trying to be himself, isn't he?"

"Yes. How are you doing?" Nicole asks, as he sets the book on the desk for Nick and turns off the reading light.

"Okay, I guess."

"Yeah, it's difficult, I know, but I think you're going to find your way too, and we'll be here if you need to come back to talk..." Nicole catches herself, tells herself to listen and not try to make things better, a weakness of hers.

"I know, but I'm still worried...." Nick says.

Nicole pulls up a chair, sits and listens as Nick talks about home and being on his own.

In another room, Matt talks to Cheryl, who has been sexually abused. "Will I ever find a man who will want and respect me?" she asks. Matt tries to assure her that she will.

Each of the themes above can be elaborated on at great length, which I often do in classes while making a few connections to volumes and articles that have been written about each, but for now it is sufficient to say that these themes in some way should be evident in the shift at Nexus, and subsequently are instrumental along with many other themes in competent youth work where the goal is to create as many moments of connection, discovery and empowerment as possible, or at least that is the central argument here. Further, while most of the themes that emerge from sketches are not new, they are new in the way they are created, combined, and seen in daily interactions in youth work, with new insights to be gained from each new occurrence of a theme.

METAPHORS FOR INTEGRATING THEMES INTO YOUTH WORK PRACTICE

In the study with youth workers (Krueger, 2004), and in several other writings, I have used metaphors such as modern dance, basketball, jazz, and conversation to frame youth work. Each of these metaphors suggests that youth work requires learning, study, practice, and improvisation during interactions. Modern dance is the one I return to most often: thinking about youth work as a dance that is choreographed (planned) in advance, according to specific themes based on the theories and practices mentioned at the beginning of the chapter, then improvising to the developmental rhythms and tempos of a shift and a group of youth, works for me. Effective youth workers it seems learn as much as they can about the dance (youth work), practice, and then learn to be rather spontaneous (improvise) in making choices about what to do, where to be, and how to move and act. In my classes, we practice two basic moves in modern dance, lining up and passing through, then we talk about any number of related issues such as body language, proximity, boundaries, use of self, etc., such as in the following sketch from a monthly column I write, Moments with Youth, for an Online, the online magazine at www.cyc-net.org:

It's near the end of my spring youth work class, which I have taught now for more than 20 years. Last week Kaseva, who grew up on a Navajo Reservation, played classical guitar, and his flute. The rest of us danced. We practiced two movements I had learned a few semesters ago from a modern dance teacher who I had invited to our class, passing through and lining-up.

As Kaseva played we wove in and out in the middle of the room. We went wherever we wanted, and surprisingly did not bump into each other. First we did this with no eye contact and then with eye contact. This was done to practice and demonstrate passing through.

Next, we lined up with each other. I stopped the group in the middle of our passing through and we lined-up with another person in a way that our body language mirrored back our impressions of that person at the time. We tried to make whatever configurations best represented what we felt about the other person, and/or ourselves in relationship to the other person. Throughout, Kaseva changed the tempo of the music, and our moods and movements automatically followed.

These two movements from modern dance, lining-up and passing through, exemplify rhythmic interactions I explained. "Youth work, as I have said many times, is like a modern dance in which we move through a day in and out of synch with youth. The challenge is to get a feel for work so we can form as many moments of connection, discovery, and empowerment as possible."

Together then we explored the relationship between what we had just done and various techniques and practices we had learned earlier in the course, such as mirroring, body language, rhythmic interaction, and proximity. I have done this before. Almost always it works as a good learning exercise. Getting up and doing something gets us in the mood for discussion, and of course lets us practice, and this in turn sheds new light on our topic.

While we were talking I said that basketball was also a good metaphor for me. Often I played three-on-three or one-on-one basketball with the youth. Similar to a modern dance we lined-up and passed through as we competed, which brought in another element for discussion, competition, its role and place in youth work. "In hindsight," I said, "It wasn't so much about competition as process. We were feeling each other out, gauging the space between us, moving toward a goal (basket), defending, facing off, facing one another, not facing one another, giving eye contact, not giving eye contact, faking, not faking, etc."

Then, the others shared their examples of things they liked to do: soccer, dancing, painting, and hoola hoops, in which they felt they had similar opportunities for rhythmic interactions, engagement, etc. At the end we had the epiphany once again that yes, this is where most of the development in our work occurs, in these interactions--whether a game or chore or sitting quietly, each moment, movement, and interaction had enormous potential.

As we talked, I smiled to myself. I was back home, where I started as a young youth worker who believed that all my interactions could be powerful if I knew what I was doing. After all these years, it still boiled down to this, something so simple, yet complex.

Then Kaseva asked if he could play his flute for us. He explained that as a young boy on the reservation he heard the Navajo play their flutes and he wanted to learn to play.

"Was it hard?" one of the class members asked.

"Sort of. But once I decide to do something with my music, I stay with it until I get it."

"It's the same with your classical guitar isn't it? You are really very good." I said.

He smiled, played his flute, and took us to another place, a very ancient, haunting place. It was beautiful. Afterwards, we talked about how music was his grand passion, and how important it was for the kids to find something they were passionate about, and us as well. "To be good at youth work you have to be passionate about it, don't you?" one of the students asked.

I smiled and said, "Yes. Remember how Kaseva made a health food dinner with the youth on his field placement. At first they didn't like it because the food was not the fast food they were used to. But then sensing Kaseva's fondness for cooking they got into it, didn't they Kaseva?"

"Yes, it took some time, but eventually they really started to like the food. But I think they liked cooking it with me even more."

Then others joined in with examples from their field placements. Time went quickly. Before we knew it, the class was over. We said, "Goodbye," and "See you next week." I packed the materials and stepped outside. It was a nice spring evening. On the way home I felt good, and sensed that the others did as well. We were on to something that was old and new.

51

No matter which metaphor or metaphors you choose, the argument is, that themes, theories, and practices, such as the ones presented earlier in the chapter, guide youth workers as they dance, play ball, converse, dine, and play together. To exemplify let's imagine that you are a youth worker like Matt or Nicole in a group home like Nexus. You begin by planning a day or shift in advance so that the opportunities for moments of connection, discovery, and empowerment are increased. In a traditional sense, you plan activities that are geared to the developmental readiness and capacity of the youth to participate. In a less traditional sense, these moments might be called your creative works. You use your imagination, ingenuity and creativity to create as many of these moments as possible, and the more a youth experiences the more likely he or she is to develop in healthy ways.

Plans and activities guide your actions, but during the day you constantly improvise. You play off the youth, letting your senses, instincts, and intuition guide you. You are in the moment, breathing, hearing, seeing, sensing your proximity to the youth, and communicating with your body, but you are always trying to be aware of how you feel and interpret what's going on and how this differs from how the youth feel and see their activity.

To create a moment of connection, discovery, and/or empowerment you raise or lower your voice, walk slow or fast, shift position, sit, stand, question, and search for common ground. You also change the beat. The story of a shift or moment changes direction with a new activity or shift in tempo and mood. Sometimes your improvisations are slightly off. Despite your best effort you are out of synch with the youth. So you try again, learning from your experience.

You respond to and shape the multiple contexts within which your interactions with youth take place (Krueger and Stuart, 1999). You are curious about the different meanings that you and the youth make of an interaction or activity. The meaning of a meal or bedtime or a walk in the park, for instance, is different for each participant. You ask, "What's it like for you?"

You are aware of the atmosphere in which an interaction or activity occurs—the tone, mood, space, light, sound, and smell. The dining room might be noisy or quiet, the play area too small or the right size for the number of participants. You dim the lights, lower your voice, and so forth.

You think about the nature of what you are doing. If the task is too difficult or not challenging enough the context is different, than when the task is challenging but not overly taxing. The nature of the activity is different when it's a shared activity rather than when it isn't a shared activity. You finger paint with a group of youth instead of using brushes and have each youth do an individual painting as opposed to a mural because this activity is more consistent with the youths' developmental capacities and readiness to participate at the moment.

You are in the world with youth in a way that allows these moments to emerge from your actions and interactions. You create moments when you are connected. We are here, you and I, together in the moment. I can feel your presence with me as we walk together or do a chore or eat a meal.

Together you discover new insights about yourselves and the world around you. Your days are filled with "ah ha" experiences. Youth say things like, "I got it. I see what you mean. I figured it out with you. Now I understand how I feel." A youth realizes that he is angry and that there is another way to express his anger. Another youth figures out how to put a decal on a model car he's making. Popcorn is made for the first time by another youth.

Finally, you create opportunities for empowerment. Youth feel and or say, "I can do it. I feel good about myself. I want to try again because I am confident that I can make it." A youth gets back on a bicycle and maintains his balance. Another youth expresses a feeling of anger for the first time. Three youth put up a tent for the first time on a camping trip.

These moments occur in multiple situations and contexts. Following are four more examples:

You approach a youth on a street corner. You are aware of your feelings— perhaps anxiety and apprehension. You hear and see what's going on. You position yourself a few feet from the youth and say hello. Normally you would look in someone else's eyes to show a sense of respect and caring, but on the street, in this neighborhood it is a sign of disrespect or "dissing" to look in someone's eyes. So you are cautious about how long you maintain eye contact with the youth as you try to make a connection. You are aware of how your presence and body language influence the situation. Your affect is firm yet open and welcoming.

A youth comes from a family or culture where he has been taught not to disclose his feelings in public or with people outside the family or community. Thus, you engage the youth in art projects and activities such as tumbling so he can express himself in other ways. You listen and watch with undivided attention trying to hear and see what the youth is saying through her or his actions.

With sensitivity to the meaning and rituals of meals, you plan a diverse menu and decorate the dining room with colors and pictures that express the diversity of the group. You learn with and from youth about mealtime in different cultures as you create a new culture for eating together. The meals are planned and paced with sensitivity to rituals, traditions, and rhythms of the participants. As you eat together, you guide the conversation and pass the food, trying to make everyone feel welcomed at the table.

Bedtime for one youth means he will have to put his head on his pillow and be alone with his thoughts of failure, rejection, and abuse. He was abused in the middle of the night and awakened by fights and the sounds of violence on the streets. With an awareness of these fears, you sit next to the bed reading quietly to the youth until he falls asleep in the comfort of his room.

This closing sketch shows youth work on a field placement and the discussion that follows:

53

Katherine, a child and youth care student on a field placement at a runaway shelter for youth, is having difficulty getting one of the youth, Rick, to clean up after dinner. He is in the language of the shelter, "non compliant."

"I'll help you Rick," Katherine (the student) says to the youth.

"I don't feel like it," the youth says.

"Maybe if we do it together it won't take so long."

Rick sits silently with his arms across his chest. Aaron, a full time worker at the shelter, who wants to date Katherine, comes on the scene and says, "What's the matter Rick, you upset because your mother put you here again?"

"Fucker!" Rick says and runs out of the room. Confused and taken back that Aaron stepped into the situation, Katherine says, "Why'd you say that, now, at this time?"

"He needs to face up to his problems."

Katherine leaves the room following Rick. Aaron follows her, "I'll get that bastard to clean up."

Katherine stops, faces Aaron, and says, "Let me handle this, okay?"

"If you think you can but don't be soft on him. He has to clean up or he's going to get restricted from his privileges."

"I know," she says and heads for his room.

"What did you do?" I ask as the professor in charge of Katherine's field placement.

"I talked quietly with him into his room. I stayed focused on getting the job done together, and eventually he came with me back to the kitchen and we cleaned up."

"Sounds like good child and youth care."

"Yes, and while we were cleaning up, he told me how angry he was about having to come back to the shelter."

"Then what did you do?"

"I asked him if he knew why he was there and he said he did but he still didn't think it was fair."

"Then what?"

"I just listened and talked with him about several things."

"Why do you think Aaron stepped in?"

"I'm not sure, maybe because he wanted to show me how tough he was?"

"Probably, but it didn't work, did it?"

"No."

"Why?"

"Because his timing and motives were off," she pauses then asks, "Why do they have all those restrictions? It seems as if every time a youth turns around he or she is getting a privilege taken away. And often it is something they need to experience to feel better about themselves, like going off grounds or participating in activities."

"It's a form of control that they are not able to provide with their presence and relationships."

"Yes, I can see that. A few of the workers rarely have to restrict the kids."
"Those are the ones to watch and learn from."

SUMMARY

Youth work is a way of being, in which workers and youth create new moments that become part of their evolving narratives and view of self. It occurs in an imperfect world with insufficient support and many competent and incompetent workers. Nonetheless, in their interactions with competent and committed workers, slowly but surely, youth's stories are filled with moments that they can continue to learn from and recall with fondness. They learn that fear and anger can be dealt with, that struggle can lead to success, and that knowing sadness is part of being happy. They also learn how to speak with one another, do chores, solve problems, and care for self. Each moment, in and of its self, is significant, and together, they create an evolving montage that guides the youth toward a more fulfilling life.

The emphasis is also on self (worker and youth) in action. The focus is on the worker and the youth in the daily living environment: worker and youth being "real," workers and youths acting with purpose and making meaning, workers and youths becoming aware, workers and youths moving in and out of synch with each other's rhythms for trusting and growing, workers and youths, moving in space, time and surroundings. Workers, through acting and being in harmony with self, while weaving care, learning, and counseling into daily interactions teach and empower youth. There is more to it, of course, but this, in my opinion, is a general definition of what child and youth care is, which of course is subject to your interpretations and meanings.

MY PRESENCE IN MULTICULTURAL YOUTH WORK

Presence is a theme in most of my sketches. Like all youth workers, I am more effective when I "show up," as a youth worker said, and am in the moment, self-aware, open and available to mirror back my experience of youth (Fewster, 1999). Similarly, in sketching, I have to be there in reflection to understand what is going on around me. This is a challenge. On one level, I have to try to remember and understand how my history influences my interactions. Or as anthropologist Sarris (1993, p. 5) wrote, about his inquiry into Pomo Indian basket weaver and medicine woman, "It is important that I remember my life, my presence, and history, as I attempt to understand Mabel. As I learn about Mabel I learn more about myself." And on another level I have to try to be "lost in the dance" the way actor Wilhem Defoe described in an interview on the TV program *Inside the Actor's Studio*, "When I'm out of my head and lost in the movement of the dance, it opens me to letting in outside influences."

My sense of it is that in youth work it is the quest to be present, that matters more than the actual amount of presence we have, at any given moment. If we are trying to be there, this seems to come across to others. Thus, in the sketches I presented earlier, I question my presence in a restraint, a stare, a run along the beach, and a moment of hesitation. Am I there, open and available, aware on some level of my history, and biases as I interact and am enmeshed in my experiences with Daniel?

MAKING MYSELF MORE VISIBLE

I believe like many others that presence transcends most differences. If people are sincere and genuine, and curious about each other's stories as they make meaning together, they will respect each other, work together, and get along. Lately, however, as I have read more about critical race theory, class, and oppression, I have been wondering how I might have directly or inadvertently contributed to hegemony. What was it I brought to those moments in youth work and my efforts to work with other youth workers to develop a profession that might have inadvertently, or directly, contributed to exclusionary, oppressive, and insensitive practices and relationships with youth?

In writing about power, class, and critical race theory in youth work, Skott-Mhyre (2006) argued that one of the problems is that workers are not visible in youth work programs and this and the literature makes it difficult to fully value youth. I am simplifying here but I believe his point was the absence of focus on workers in a field that was trying to focus on youth involvement and agency created an equation for progress in which half was missing. Therefore we were more or less destined to failure as a field just as relationships are destined to failure when only one person is participating. In short, Skott-Mhyre (2006), in proposing a radical, post Marxist, grass roots, worker/youth-focused model of youth work, argued for the importance of presence again. Thus, I wrote the following personal narrative to explore my history and make myself more visible.

MY PATH TO AND IN YOUTH WORK: JOURNEY AS THE WRONG METAPHOR?

My older brother and I were the sons of parents from German families that like most German families in Milwaukee had abandoned most of their culture during two world wars. Suffice it to say it was not popular to be German in those days in America, (1940s and 1950s), and so most of these families pretended not to be, some even changed their names or the pronunciation of their names. Krueger (Krooger), for example, became Kreeger. German, which had been the primary language in the schools before WWI, was rarely spoken in public, and not at all in our house.

We lived in a duplex in a lower middle class neighborhood on the Northwest Side with blue and white collar families. Our friends were largely Italian, Greek, and Jewish. Strangely, we did not talk much about the war, or even know much about it and our parents,' relatives, and ancestors' conflicts. This was "not our business." Maybe others talked about it in their homes, I'm not sure. We didn't in ours. For the Jewish kids', the Sabbath was on Saturday and their houses and Italians' houses, looked and smelled different inside than our house. Those were the major differences as far as I was concerned. Oh, and the Jewish girls were not to date the gentiles, although most of them did.

Racial slurs and jokes were not used at home. My parents had been "dirt poor" as kids and somehow emerged from it without the overt biases and prejudices that I saw on the playgrounds. My father called the women at work, who were mostly secretaries, "gals" but that was about the extent of what I heard from my parents that today might be considered derogatory, sexist or racist.

At the time "colored people" were in increasing numbers moving north for the city's high paying blue collar jobs in industry. My father, who often told me stories about how rough he had had it as a poor kid, once said, "It would have been much more difficult if I were a colored person." There were few children of color in our school. I went to the black section of town to play basketball and listen to music. We were not afraid to go into the black community, at least I wasn't. Parents and adults, black and white, seemed to watch out for us.

For the past few years, Milwaukee like many cities in the U.S., has been in a state of decline. Many of the good paying jobs are gone. A few weeks ago, I rode back to my old neighborhood to see if this had an impact. Most of the once neat and tidy little houses and frame duplexes were run down. Young black men walked the streets. A couple stepped in front of my car and "dissed" me. (Milwaukee graduates less than 35% of the African American men from high school.) Three young black women sat on our porch steps with young children. (Milwaukee has one of the highest rates of teen pregnancy in the U.S.) When I pulled into the alley and rode behind my old house, I was frightened. A satellite dish had replaced our basketball backboard and hoop on the garage roof. Garbage had not been picked up. It was very different yet I felt a sort of odd kinship with a young man who stared at me over a fence.

As I described in Chapter 1, when I grew up there, most of the families seemed to want to forget and escape into the *American Pastoral* as Phillip Roth later called it in his Pulitzer Prize winning novel (Roth, 1997) about those times. My father worked for the same life insurance company all his life, hardly ever missing a day. My mother had been a "flapper," who smoked, drove and worked, long before it was popular. They worked their way out of poverty and through the depression to the middle class, waiting to have children until they could afford it. They were in their mid thirties.

While I worked with youth, I joined with other youth workers in an effort to form a profession. Together, black, brown, men, women, we organized, spoke out, and wrote about our importance to youth and society. We did not see ourselves as an oppressed class but rather revolutionaries who were going to change the "fucking," excuse the language, youth work world. There were the usual tensions, power struggles, differences (geographical, racial, cultural developmental), but on the whole we respected and valued each other, perhaps because of what we learned from and about working with kids and civil rights.

We stayed away from labels with the kids and ourselves. Terms like "white privilege" would not have been used other than perhaps in the context of humor because white privilege would have stigmatized someone just as other labels did (Magnet, 2006). We were well aware of the inequities associated with the color of a persons' skin and the history of racism in the country. Jane Adams, Martin Luther King Jr., Gandhi, Maclolm X, Angela Davis, Joan Baez, Huey Newton, Robert Kennedy, George McGovern, Eugene McCarthy, Saul Alinsky, and Caesar Chavez had been our influences (in my case taking on more importance after I found my cause), and we wanted to move on while recognizing and trying to rectify disparities in class, race, etc. that made it more challenging for the youth and some of us.

Looking back, you could say we wanted to maintain the innocence of our struggle in which despite our different races, cultures, and classes (*Daniel as my symbol of the struggle with youth*), we had found something similar that called to all of us in our brotherhood and sisterhood for the cause (Magnet, 2006). After three black presidents I became the first white president of our national association, and was followed by a gay president. We made progress in developing a knowledge base for our field, and in showing how practice with youth could be improved. We raised the standards in many states and countries for practice, developed bachelors, masters and Ph.D. programs, and increased cross-cultural sensitivity and awareness in our field. Many of us seized the opportunities in our

59

emerging profession and advanced our careers. Some went on to high level appointments in government. Others became executive directors of youth serving agencies. Many became superb practitioners. I became a professor and founded a research and education center for youth workers.

Yet, salaries, support, preparation, and working conditions, on average for youth workers, did not improve that much, if at all. In some places the work was done better than ever, but in comparison to other industrialized countries (generalizations are always difficult), we did not do very well, in part because of cuts in funding for programs for youth. Youth, and particularly youth of color, continued to be exposed to the risks and challenges that made it difficult for them to develop and succeed in our society. Some would argue that things, with the exception of a few upswings, actually got worse during this period for youth and youth workers.

My colleagues and I often wondered why? Were we too idealistic? Were we wrong to focus on knowing ourselves in a way that genuinely opened us to others with the hope they would do the same for us? Had we underestimated the power of racism, hegemony, and white privilege? Were we too self-serving and not youth focused enough? Was it because our voice was not loud enough? As the distribution of wealth widened and more youth were impoverished, why were we, like other human service groups, losers in the political, social and economic debates?

Lately, I have been second guessing myself, partially because of the trip back to my neighborhood, which I mentioned earlier. I wonder if I hadn't missed something all along. When a black friend, who preceded me as president, insisted on not sitting with his back to the door in a restaurant, should I have been more sensitive to my white privilege, racism, profiling, and how it influenced the way he saw the world. When we were refused entry into a Florida nightclub because of our dress when two young white men had just entered in T shirts, and he smiled at me, had I underestimated how much of an impact this had on his and other youth and workers of color attitudes about life and our efforts to change things? Should I have listened more to my father when he told me his trip out of poverty would have been much more difficult if he "were colored?" I thought I had but maybe not with sufficient understanding.

Were we, as self-styled revolutionaries, naive about how engrained racism and prejudice were in relationship to youth work, a racially mixed profession whose membership in many urban communities today is predominantly African American or Latino? Had we (I) not been able to see the neutralizing powers of our collective experiences in a country that is predominantly white? Were we not as sensitive to these issues as we had thought we were? I don't know.

Did I overlook, for example, how much this meant to boys like Daniel, in the novel I wrote about youth work (Krueger, 1987)? How it influenced their world view and interpreted how I interacted with them? Did I miss something hidden in my profession, and/or community? Did we miss something that was hidden in our multicultural curriculum and activities and instead suppress the very initiatives we were trying to undertake (Jay, 2003)? And/or was it just all part of living in a country that has never really valued people who work with other peoples' children, and children without families? In capitalism will youth always play second fiddle to war and profit (McNaughton, 2006; Skott-Mhyre & Gretzinger, 2005)? Or was it just simply about racism in a society with widening class divisions in which people of color always seem disproportionately to wind up on the short end of the stick?

I have also been wondering if journey was the wrong metaphor as Halse (2006, pp 105-106) recently articulated in her argument that as an interpretive device in Western autobiography, "journey" tends not to reflect what it purports to represent. Had we deceived ourselves by framing our work as a *shared* journey into believing something other than what was occurring, and by believing something other than what was occurring inadvertently clouding our arguments and steering our focus from the reality of the moment, past and present?

Anyway, these are the types of questions some members of our field and I have been openly asking. We don't necessarily have an answer to these questions other than perhaps all of the above as it applies on a case by case basis. Meanwhile, to remain optimistic some of us have told ourselves we are doing fairly well in comparison to other professions at similar stages of development. Whether or not in the ebb and flow of these political, economic, and social tides, our approach will have impact is yet to be seen, but we continue the struggle, naively perhaps, with the hope that it will as long as we are in it together and able to question ourselves.

THE TOUR: A WORK IN PROGRESS

In my continued exploration of the questions and themes above, I have been working for a while on a sketch that I will call here, "The Tour," based on a visit to a largely Hispanic and African American populated community where Carlos, based on one of my former students, works, and was "practically raised." The center is near the house where my father grew up "dirt-poor." Perhaps I should say up front that Carlos is Latino, and that I grew up as I described a moment ago in a German American family. As I have gotten older, more and more I have been longing to know this part of me that is missing.

I arrive early. Carlos greets me at the door. It's about 8:30 PM. A number of youth are still in the main room.

"Hi Carlos," I say. As usual, he looks good, polished in a nice sport coat with a crew neck sweater.

Two teenagers run out the door.

Carlos gives me the latest handshake, which includes bumping my fist with his fist. I fumble, never quite sure what the new one is.

"You look mighty fine," I joke.

"Have to, otherwise I can't get money from the suits downtown." Unlike most youth workers, Carlos is usually dressed up. He dresses this way to "serve as a role model." He is the senior worker at the center and in his words, "runs the

place. "*Everyone knows Carlos,*" *is the typical response in the neighborhood and much of the Milwaukee youth work community.*

"*My father grew up in this neighborhood,*" *I say.*

"*Man, that must have been ancient times,*" *he smiles.*

I grin and say, "*It was mostly German and Polish families in those days.*"

"*I've heard that--Mostly Latino, Hmong, and African American around here now.*"

*

(1919) My father, 12, and uncle, 13, walk down the street looking, as they used to say, as if they had cement in their deodorant. They have just finished the collections for their paper routes. Five Polish boys approach.

"*What do you Huns have in there?*" *The biggest Polish boy points to a small sack my uncle is carrying.*

"*Nothing,*" *my father says.*

"*Lets see?*" *The big Polish boy steps toward them.*

"*Back off!*" *my uncle says.*

The Polish boys begin to circle, fists clenched.

My father and uncle stand back to back and fight them off, so the story goes.

*

"*If you have a connection at United Way put in a word for us,*" *Carlos says changing the subject.*

"*I have.*"

"*Thanks.*"

"*Are you still doing the cleaning at night?*" *I ask.*

He nods, "*Every night after we close. Stop by some night and give us a hand.*"

"*I will,*" *I say, embarrassed. Carlos invited me at least twice before.*

"*Yeah, we still got a lot of work to do to get this place the way I want it.*"

"*The big main room has a mural and several game tables—air hockey, pool, foosball. Some kids mill around, others are engaged in these activities with youth workers. A girl, maybe 16, runs up to Carlos. He hugs her. My eyebrows rise.*

Several boys are standing around a wood platform about the size of a boxing ring clapping their hands to Hip Hop music.

"*Look at this.*" *Carlos walks ahead. One of the boys is spinning on his back on the linoleum floor of the platform, which is about four inches above the ground. He's really good.*

"*These are our break dancers,*" *Carlos says.*

"*I heard about them. They dance at intermission for the Bucks basketball games, don't they?*"

"*Yes.*"

*

A few years earlier, I attend the rally. We are protesting a referendum for sales tax to build a domed stadium for the Milwaukee Brewers. Our main argument is that the community would not support a sales tax to improve the schools; why should we use tax dollars to support a sports team that charges ticket prices that poor kids can't afford to pay.

*

The dancers are fantastic. They have incredible moves, moves I can't even imagine doing. But more important, they are well mannered and behaved. Carlos insists on it otherwise they can't participate.

"Jose! Get your hands off her," Carlos says and swipes his open hand across the top of Jose's head. He looks at me anticipating what I might say. "My hand was open, man. He knows I care about him."

"Still..."

"I know, I know. We talked about it in class....These computers were donated." Carlos opens the door to one of the side rooms off the main floor. I look in. The room is packed.

"What are they doing?"

"Searching the web. Playing games. Most of these kids don't have computers at home."

*

"We had hope. We were poor, dirt poor, poorer even than the families that live in that neighborhood now, but we thought if we worked hard we would get someplace. That's gone now," says my father to me when I tell him about how hard it is for some of the kids.

"But you worked all your life for the same company. Is that what you dreamed for?"

"You didn't live through the Depression."

*

One of the teenage girls is on a cell phone. She's leaning against the wall with her midriff exposed and her pants low on her hip. A smaller boy runs up and hugs Carlos around the waist. "What are you going to get me for my birthday?" he asks.

"What do you want?"

"Nintendo."

*

About ten eager students arrive by about 9:30 p.m. The youth workers on duty and Carlos say goodbye to the last of the youth as they close up for the night. We start a group discussion, but once Carlos has the stage it's hard for him to let go. When a student asks him about something she read in our class, he jokes about how school isn't helpful on the streets. "Books can't tell you what it's like, even your's right professor?" he jokes with me. Then he gets serious and challenges their commitment, almost to the point of being in their faces, or "of being obnoxious" as one student puts it in class the following week. "What you doing for your community? Nothing probably. You have to live this stuff...Get your coats. I'll show you."

We follow him outside. A light mist hangs over the poor, rough neighborhood. "The neighbors are trying to make it a safe place," Carlos explains as he walks ahead with what we used to call a swagger. My parents would have called him a dandy. He has the walk and talk down.

*

On Friday, Joy and I talked
about sense of presence.
What is it? How does it come about?
I think it has to do with worth, dignity,
and how you fit with ocassion, place,
people and time.
It is also a physical thing
carriage of body,
hand and head movements,
eyes fixed upon specific points.
And then it is an ability
Which is instinctive and spiritual
To convey what you see
To those around you.
Essentially, it is how you fit
Into the space which is yourself
How well and appropriately...

From "Four Deeseyahmah Poems" by Simon Ortiz (1992, p. 128)

*

When we cross the main street, two policemen in a squad car stop in the middle of the road.

"Hey, Carlos, come here," The cop on the passenger side calls him over. Carlos circles with his arm for us to cross the street and walks over and speaks with them a few minutes. After the squad leaves Carlos says, "I'm a bridge between the gangs and the police. Both accept me.

"Are you a snitch?" a male student asks.

"No. Don't ask don't tell is our rule. They don't ask me things that will put me in danger with the gang, and I don't tell them." A few months ago he told me he thought he knew who shot a young lady in the community and he suspected the police knew he knew but they didn't ask him because they didn't want to set him up *as a snitch. He was too valuable as someone who was trying to get kids out of the gangs. They knew if he were identified as a snitch he'd have to move. Fortunately, they caught the gang member who did the shooting, but I couldn't help but wonder what I would have done in Carlos' shoes.*

Carlos says hello to a woman who is standing in her frontyard looking at the stars.

"What you looking at?"

"The stars, but I don't think we'll be able to see them, not in the city with all these street lights."

Carlos looks up, "No, probably not tonight."

We continue our walk. A car with four teens in it, "gang bangers," stops in an alleyway that crosses the street. Carlos walks to the car, exchanges hand greetings, puts one arm on top of the car, and leans in. "What are you dudes doing on the streets? You should be home doing homework."

They give him a little heat. "I'm serious," he says and taps on top of the car.

They drive off. We continue our walk. "Let's go in here." Carlos climbs the porch steps of a bungalow and rings the doorbell. We follow apprehensively. "It's okay. I know her!" he waves us forward.

An older woman answers. Carlos speaks to her and she invites us in. We stand in a circle in her dining room, surrounded by boxes of plastic garbage bags. Carlos explains that she is a community leader, a person everyone trusts and respects. Heavyset with a permanent smile on her face she speaks proudly and energetically about the neighborhood and how fond she is of Carlos and how far he has come since his rough childhood. Carlos beams. She offers us a can of pop (a soft drink). A few students accept.

"The police donate the pop and these plastic bags," she says, pointing to boxes of large trash bags.

"What's it for?" one of the students asks.

"The children," she says. "I want them to feel they can come here any time and get a can of pop and a plastic bag to pick up trash in the neighborhood. That's how we build community. The police stop here too."

"How long have you lived here?" a student asks.

"All my life."

"Why didn't you leave?" another student asks.

"Because it's my home."

She invites us to come back on the weekend to clean up with her. A few students eagerly accept the invitation. Carlos walks us back to our cars. I thank him and tell the students we will talk about our visit next week. They seem impressed and a bit frightened by what they have experienced; their initial impressions of Carlos as a cocky, in your face, worker, changed, perhaps.

*

On my way home, I wonder what my father would have thought about the neighborhood today. I think he would have been disappointed that it was still rough and poor, but he would have liked the diversity. I do. We marched across the bridge in the sixties to integrate the neighborhood. Polish people were waiting with shotguns, but no one got hurt. I stop in front of the house where my father was raised. It seems so small. He told me a story once about how when he was a boy he wanted to go to camp but they couldn't afford it. Then one day he was digging with his toes in the back yard and he found a coin purse with a several dollar bills, just enough to go to camp. His mother made him put an ad in the newspaper to see if anyone would claim it (that was good community work) and when no one did, he got to go to camp.

Later, after my mother had died and he was living alone in another part of town, someone broke into the house. They took the TV set, some silverware, and the coin purse. He felt totally violated. He didn't care about the TV or the silverware. "But why'd they have to take the coin purse? It's worth nothing to them," he said. Nonetheless, he continued volunteering his time for causes he thought would make the community stronger. As I drive away I remember how as a boy he used to turn on streetlights with a long pole and then I think of the woman trying to see the stars.

*

"So would you tell?" I ask a student in class the week after we go on the tour of the neighborhood.

"Tell what?"

"If you were in Carlos' position, and you knew someone in a gang or the hood that committed a crime, would you tell the police?"

"No, that would be snitching."

"That's not ethical. You have an obligation to report the crime," another student responds.

"Even if it means you put yourself and your family at risk?" I ask.

"What do you mean?"

"Well I suppose if he tells, the gang or the offenders will retaliate and he will either have to move out of the community or allow himself or his family to be at risk of retaliation. Right now he's a very valuable member of the community who has helped several young people out of gangs. But if he's identified as a snitch, he will no longer be able to do that, will he?"

"I guess not. What would you do?" the students ask me.

"I don't know. I'd like to think I'd let my conscience be my guide and do the right thing, but if I were in Carlos' shoes, I don't know what would be right?"

"Puts things in another perspective, doesn't it?" another student says…

In this sketch, constructed from several fragments, I try to see and read Carlos as it relates to my experience and history. I try to understand his power and presence in his interactions with the youth, workers, and members of the neighborhood within the larger social, cultural and political environments in which these interactions take place. I read his actions, in part, as they are determined by the politics, culture, and norms of the neighborhood and community, and, in part, through the lens of my history and experience.

At this point, I shall leave further interpretation up to the reader and finish my discussion by saying I have come to believe that it is this process of exploration, perhaps more than anything else that is successful multicultural youth work: the ability to be open to, question, and learn from my personal experiences and the experiences of other.

In closing I offer this poem I have worked on, on and off, for several years.

Migrants

There is something romantic
about seeing the parents and children
hunched over in the fields

the easy pace of their hard work
the cranes overhead
with their ancient wings
pushing against time

A hard life but together
much of the time in the fields

At the end of the day
I see them again
at Antique Liquor:

> The kids and mothers
> picking through video boxes
> with pictures of heroes and villains
> with enough firepower
> to blow them and the fields
> where they work to smithereens

> And the fathers lined-up
> with whiskey bottles,
> the smell from last nights fill
> still seeping out of their clothes
> with the strawberries and cucumbers

With a selection of my own
dramas in hand
the rusty pickups
pull onto the highway

with the kids in back

> And remember how I waited
> for a man with his dark hair slicked
> back to get off a bus
> the doors opening and closing
> opening and closing
> day fading with each gasp of air

I want to tell them the odds
are against them but don't

I too once found solace
in a good days' work

It was the late afternoons
that were hardest

> From 4:00 PM on:
> when I lingered
> in the downdraft
> and fed my dreams
> with the taste of dusk

The doors opening and closing
like the doors of Antique Liquor
around sunset on a summer night

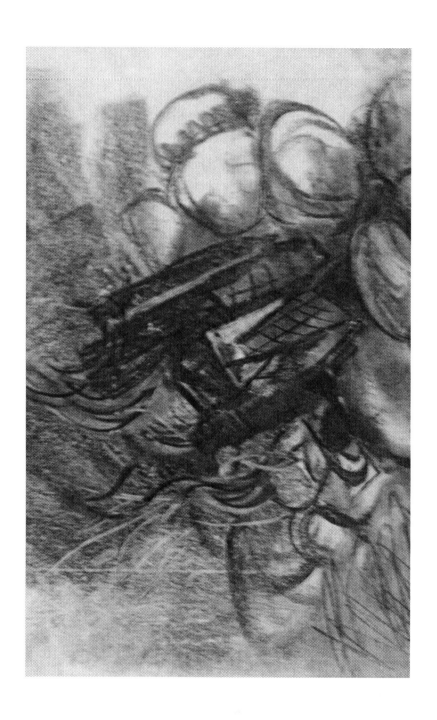

THE TEAM MEETING: *A THREE ACT PLAY*

The following play was created from a number of sketches of team meetings I attended.

Characters:
SHANTELL: A child and youth care worker (26 years old)
RICARDO: A child and youth care worker (30)
ANGIE: A child and youth care worker (20)
BILL: The overnight worker (24)
CAMILLE: The clinical social worker (40)
TONY: The child and youth care supervisor (35)

Act I

THE SETTING: The boardroom at a residential treatment center in a large city. All of the characters are seated around the table. A rhomboid of light is shining through a window, like in the opening scene of Beckett's Endgame. *No walls or doors. The background is dark except for the light from the window that shines on the characters and on the table. Books are on a shelf opposite from the window through which children can be heard playing outside. A small overhead lamp shines on the books, a collection of classics in child and youth care work. The curtain rises. We enter the middle of the meeting. They are talking about the eight boys in their cottage.*

SHANTELL (*Determined. Her dark eyes shining, body straight in the chair, eyes focused first on one, then the other, as she speaks*): We need more consistency and structure. The kids are getting away with murder. They know how to play us against one another.
RICARDO (*Slouched back in his chair*): That's not realistic.
ANGIE (*Curious*): What isn't realistic?
RICARDO: To be consistent and structured all the time. It's not the way we live our lives and relate to others. The kids know right away. They have to learn what it's like in the real world.
BILL (*Bookish*): And where would that be?
RICARDO: What do you mean?
BILL: The real world, what real world are you talking about, the one they experience or the one you experience?
RICARDO (*Sarcastically*): Very clever, Mr. Philosopher. I know we all make

different meaning of our experiences. What I meant is that, in life outside the center, people aren't coming around consistently enforcing rules, and handing out consequences and rewards.

CAMILLE (*Professional*): Yes, there's some truth to that, but these are not ordinary circumstances. These kids have lived very unstructured lives and have seen the extremes of unpredictability from parents who are very permissive one moment and abusive the next. They also have been bounced around from one place to another and need to know there are some places with structure, routine, and adults they can count on to respond in firm and caring ways.

RICARDO (*Argumentative*): Bull. I grew up in a real unpredictable environment, and I turned out okay.

SHANTELL (*Angry*): I can't believe you guys are falling for this. He does it all the time just to cover up for the way he breaks the rules we establish together. Besides he didn't have it anywhere near as tough as the kids we work with.

RICARDO (*Staring at Shantell*): I had it plenty tough. You couldn't have survived a day in the world I grew up in. *Pause, Shantell turns away. Sensing she won't take the bait, Ricardo says,* Give me one example of a rule I broke.

SHANTELL (*Still not taking the bait*): So you can debate with us some more and see if you can get a rise out of us?

RICARDO (*Grinning*): No. I really want to know.

SHANTELL: Okay, last night you let the kids stay up late again. Bill told me this morning.

RICARDO (*Looks at Bill*). Is that true?

BILL (*Slightly embarrassed*): Yes, the kids were still running around after you left, and they told me you let them stay up to watch the movie.

RICARDO (*Confronting*): Next time tell me to my face.

BILL (*Reactive*): I just did.

RICARDO: First, before you tell someone else, especially her. *Looks at Shantell*

SHANTELL: So is it true?

RICARDO: Yes, it's true. We were all sitting and watching the movie and I decided we could make an exception.

SHANTELL: What kind of message does that give?

RICARDO: That I am a real human being and that I make decisions based on their Needs in the current circumstances.

ANGIE: I can see that, but aren't you worried that they will think they can get away with stuff with you?

RICARDO: Get away with what? Having a nice, calm, quiet evening together watching a good movie and eating popcorn.

SHANTELL: There's a place for that, but not when we have a rule about bedtime. You know they need time to get ready to go to sleep and you set up Bill by not following the rules.

RICARDO: Bill can defend himself, can't you Bill?

BILL: I'm not sure I have anything to defend. The kids were wild and that's a fact.

Whether or not it was because you let them stay up or you didn't settle them down doesn't seem to matter much. You still left me with a mess.

RICARDO: Why didn't you come to me first?

BILL: I was going to, but then Shantell raised the issue. I had to tell her this morning, because the kids were unusually slow and crabby.

RICARDO: She would.

SHANTELL: What?

RICARDO: Raise the issue here before coming to me.

TONY (*Speaking for the first time. Voice firm, authoritative. Chair back from the table. Legs crossed at the knees*): What movie did you watch?

RICARDO: Braveheart

TONY: That's pretty violent isn't it?

RICARDO: Yes, but it's also about heroes and freedom and what it means to stand up for what you believe.

CAMILLE (*Speaking for the first time, clinical*): Given what these children have been through, do you think it advisable to give them the message that violence is a way of becoming a hero and standing up for what you believe?

RICARDO: Look, it's a violent world out there. They know it and I know it. So why should we skirt around it. Braveheart was violent only in response to violence. Some things are worth fighting for.

CAMILLE: So responding to violence with violence is okay if you're on the right side?

RICARDO: Basically.

CAMILLE: So do you think our children have a clear picture of what is right and wrong violence?

RICARDO: Well, just by the way you use the term violence you make it seem as if any form of aggression is wrong, even self-defense.

CAMILLE: And do you think they can sort out self-defense from other forms of violence?

RICARDO: No, but they are learning.

CAMILLE: Is there another way to learn that?

TONY: Excuse me, but I have to interrupt. This is an important discussion that I don't think we can resolve now, and there are many other things to talk about.

ANGIE (*determined to make her point*): Before we move on, I just want to respond to Camille. I think there is. What about Gandhi and Martin Luther King Jr.?

RICARDO: Oh give me a break. These kids would be dead in a moment it they tried to be like those guys on the streets. Malcolm X is a better role model in my mind. Maybe Che'.

CAMILLE: I think Angie is using Gandhi and King as examples of how we can resolve conflicts in nonviolent ways. They were just as brave, if not braver, than people you mentioned.

RICARDO: And where did it get them? They were killed just like the others.

BILL (*Contemplative*). In my philosophy classes, we've been talking about morality, power, and culture, and it seems that all social political ideologies are corrupt when it comes to the development of the self. Ultimately, one becomes polarized in one form or another by their rigid beliefs and values. It might be better to just think of this for what it is, in and of itself, without bringing in all this other stuff.

RICARDO: So what are you saying? That we should just leave people be as is and everything will work out?

BILL (*Somewhat paternalistically*): No Ricardo, that we should just look at the situation without trying to apply so much groupthink.

CAMILLE (*Frustrated*): We are missing the point!

TONY: Which is?

CAMILLE: That these children all have serious emotional problems and that we have to examine the effects of our activities and relationships with them on a case by case basis. But in general we have to be very sensitive to how they interpret acts of violence, especially since most of our youth who have been sexually and physically abused.

BILL: That's what I was trying to say.

CAMILLE: Yes, but in a philosophical rather than developmental way.

BILL: What's wrong with that?

CAMILLE: There's nothing wrong with existentialism other than it makes it difficult for us, as a group, to review our cases in a way that everyone can understand.

TONY: Okay, okay, I'm sorry Bill, Ricardo, Angie and Camille, but I think we have to move on. This discussion is moving away from our agenda.

SHANTELL (*Determined*): Without resolving whether it was okay for Ricardo to let the kids stay up late?

TONY (*Sighs, looks slightly frustrated about how his agenda has been interrupted again*): I guess we should. Based on what I know I can respect what Ricardo says about the need not to be too trapped in rigid rules. I also think I get a sense of what he is saying it takes to be a man and to be able defend yourself and what you believe in. I also understand, however, what Camille said about the need for structure and predictability, and Shantell's concern about the message it gives the kids. In this case, it is my opinion that, it probably was not a good idea. Given what you watched and how you left right when your shift ended, I think you set Bill up for a rough night, and that your judgment about the movie was a little weak. If you had had time to process all the violence in that rather long movie, it might have served a better purpose, but this did not seem like the right context.

RICARDO: Figures

TONY: What

RICARDO: You're playing the culture card. Hispanic males are machismo. They see these things differently than you Anglos, and you don't like it.

TONY: Oh com'on. This has nothing to do with being machismo.

RICARDO: It doesn't? Well, then why are you trying to win?

TONY: I'm not trying to win. I'm just trying to resolve this situation. *Tony pauses, then looks Ricardo directly in the eyes.* You know what I think?

RICARDO: What?

TONY: That for some reason you are creating this power struggle with the team, and you'll keep it going as long as we let you. Maybe you and I can talk afterwards, but for now I want to hear what the others think and move on.

SHANTELL: I agree with Tony.

ANGIE (*The peacemaker*): Maybe we can set aside some time to discuss these issues in more depth. I'd like to learn more. I think several points that were made were valid.

CAMILLE (*As if still seething at what Ricardo said*): I'd like to be part of that discussion.

BILL (*As if obligated*): Me too.

TONY (*Sitting straight now, looking at his watch*): Okay, I'll set something up. Let's move on.

Act II:

Setting: Curtain pulls back again on the team meeting. It could be the same meeting or another one. All the players are present around the conference table in the conference room at the residential treatment center. Lighting and props, the same as in Scene I.

ANGIE (*Shyly*): One of the kids asked me yesterday if I slept with my boyfriend.

CAMIILE (*Cautiously inquisitive*): Did you respond?

ANGIE: Yes.

CAMILLE: What did you say?

ANGIE: Well, nothing at first, but they started to giggle and ask questions about how we did it.

TONY (*Alarmed*): Did you tell them?

ANGIE: No. I said I didn't think it was appropriate to talk about that, and I asked them to get back to our discussion about their sexual feelings. But I'm not sure I did the right thing, because they started to get silly.

CAMILLE: And what do you think was the right thing?"

ANGIE: Well, that's what I'm confused about. I never know how much of myself to disclose.

CAMILLE: And you don't think you reveal yourself all the time in the way you express your emotions?

ANGIE: Well yes, but I don't necessarily talk about it.

TONY: Why?

ANGIE: Because we're here to help them with their feelings, not ours.

CAMILLE: Is that so?

ANGIE: I think so.

BILL: So it's not important that we understand and are in touch with our feelings?

75

ANGIE: Well, yes, I suppose it is. How can we ask them to be in touch with their feelings if we're not in touch with our feelings?

CAMILLE: I agree.

ANGIE: So how much do you tell them?

SHANTELL: I don't think we should tell them much. We're not in therapy, they are. Besides, my business is my business.

RICARDO: I tell the kids a lot.

TONY: Like what?

RICARDO: Like what it was like when I was a gang member.

BILL: Why do you tell them that?

RICARDO: To let them know that I know what it is like for them. That I've been there and can relate to how they are feeling.

TONY: Have you really been there?

RICARDO: Where?

TONY: Where they have been?

RICARDO: I just said I was.

TONY: Yeah, but I mean, can you ever experience what someone else experiences?

RICARDO: Sure.

BILL: No, you can't (philosophical again). We all experience the world differently based on our past and current experiences. There is no one reality or shared experience.

RICARDO: Don't give me that bull. I know what it's like?

TONY: Maybe you know what it's like for you, but not for them.

RICARDO: So what are you saying?

TONY: Your experience of being in a gang is not their experience of being in a gang. If you understand what it was like for you, that's good, but it should also open you up to wanting to understanding what it was like for them. Otherwise, it robs them of the chance to be able to express their fears, guilt, etc., about being in a gang.

ANGIE: Can we get back to my issue?

CAMILLE: Yes, let's talk about that some more. In situations when kids ask us difficult questions about things like drugs, sex, etc. how much should we reveal?

BILL: Well, I read in one book that it's better to be open than closed, but in another book I read that we really should not share our histories.

ANGIE: I know that's what makes it so confusing.

SHANTELL: Look, I was abused as I kid too, but I got over it. I tell the kids this straight up. That's why they connect with me, because I can show them they can get over it.

CAMILLE: Let's look at it from the perspective Tony just presented. The important thing is that we understand and value our experiences and don't impose them on others, but rather let them open us and make us curious about wanting to understand the children's feelings.

ANGIE: So, we should tell them everything?

CAMILLE: No, that's not what I was trying to say. What I meant was that our awareness is revealed in the way we present ourselves, and if the kids know we understand our feelings and this opens us to understanding their feelings, they usually do not need to probe further. But, if they sense our lack of awareness, they will keep us on the hot seat, because they won't feel comfortable opening up to us.

ANGIE: That's difficult, to be like that.

CAMILLE: How?

ANGIE: So sure of how you feel.

TONY: It sure is. But I think it's not so much about how aware you are as it is about your willingness to be self-aware. The kids know that we are not perfect and don't understand all our feelings, but if they sense we are trying, they are more likely to feel safe with us and open up.

BILL: I like the way you put that.

RICARDO: I don't. This is just a bunch of mumbo jumbo. The kids need us to be strong, certain, not navel gazers.

SHANTELL: I agree with Ricardo. We have to show them we are strong, not wishy-washy. They need strong role models, not people who are always questioning themselves.

RICARDO: Wow, she agrees with me for once.

SHANTELL: It's also a cultural thing. In my family we learned not to reveal our feelings to the outside world. It's the same for the Hmong and Native American kids here. It's disrespectful of the family, tribe, and elders, to do that.

RICARDO: What have you been doing, reading another one of those books about culture? In my world there's only one culture, the culture of the street.

ANGIE: I thought you said you were machismo. That's a Hispanic thing isn't it?

RICARDO: (*Smiles at Angie*): You got me.

BILL: I agree, culture does influence how we express ourselves, but I don't think we can assume that culture influences all people the same. I know lots of Native American, Hmong and African American people, who are very open about their feelings. The key is to be aware of how their and our histories influence the way we interact. There are also many other reasons, such as temperament, that determine how open we are.

ANGIE: It's all so complicated. I'm confused about what's the right thing to do?

RICARDO: I think you are all in your heads too much. You're trying to intellectualize this thing. What you got to do is just be who you are. That's what the kids relate to.

CAMILLE: I agree Ricardo, but what does that mean?

RICARDO: It means that you are in touch.

TONY: With what?

RICARDO: With who you are, man?

ANGIE: But how can you be so certain?

RICARDO: By just being and not asking so many questions, and acting with pride and dignity.

CAMILLE: Is it that simple? Isn't there a sense of false pride and dignity that
      comes from a lack of self-questioning and awareness?

RICARDO: So what are you saying, that I'm not in touch?

CAMILLE: No, I'm just asking.

RICARDO: Just like a social worker, answering a question with a question.

CAMILLE (*Smiles*): I just don't know how you can be so sure of yourself.

RICARDO: That's because you aren't.

TONY: Okay, so I think we've gone as far as we can with this for now. Let's move
      on.

ANGIE: But I still don't feel my question was answered.

CAMILLE (*Still seething a little from Ricardo's last response*). There might not be
      one right answer. It's all situational. In one situation it's proper to talk
      about something and in another it's proper to just reveal your feelings by
      the way you are in the moment. The kids can usually tell.

ANGIE: But how do you know what's right in one situation and not another?

BILL: Look, we are all often confused, except for maybe Ricardo
      (*said sarcastically*).The key is to continually want to know your self and
      to practice. Talking like this helps, I think.

SHANTELL: I think a lot of this talk is a waste of time. Gets us no place. If you
      don't know who you are you shouldn't be working here.

TONY: Okay, time. This discussion to be continued.

ACT III

*SCENE: Once again, all the characters are seated in the boardroom--the position of
the characters and the angle of the shadows from the sun have changed. The voices
of children outdoors are softened. There is the sound of a woman washing coffee
cups in the small kitchen off the boardroom. She hears the conversation, stops,
stands, and listens out of sight.*

BILL: Nikki (one of the girls), asked me to rub her back last night.

SHANTELL (*Alarmed*): Did you do it?

BILL: Yes.

SHANTELL: Do you think that's right?

BILL: I'm not sure, that's why I raised it.

SHANTELL: Well, I think it sends the wrong message.

CAMILLE: And what might that be.

SHANTELL: It's too sexual.

CAMILLE: Does it have to be?

SHANTELL: Well, I don't see how she can take it any other way, especially after
      the abuse she's received from men.

BILL: But fathers and caring men do it all the time with younger children. Seems
      like it's a very natural thing to do to show care and affection. And it's
      probably what she needs more than anything else.

SHANTELL: What?

BILL: To be touched by a caring man.

TONY: Bill, you used the word natural. My question is, natural to who, you or them?

BILL: Well, that's a good question. I suppose it depends on what you have dxperienced. But if you've never experienced normal caring touch, how do you get to experience it if someone isn't willing to take the risk to try, especially today when men are being sued and accused of wrong doing all the time by kids. I heard at some places you can't even touch the kids. To me that's absurd. How can you connect if you can't touch? Touch is fundamental to healthy development.

CAMILLE: I would agree, but is a backrub with Nikki the proper place to start?

BILL: Depends, I guess, on how she takes it.

TONY: And how do you think she took the backrub?

BILL: Appropriately, I think.

TONY: Based on what you felt or she felt?

BILL: My sense of both, I think. But I guess I should talk to her.

ANGIE (*Looking as if she did something wrong*): My God, I hug the boys all the time. Is that wrong?

CAMILLE: I think what we just discussed with Bill applies with hugs as well. What does that kind of touch mean, and given what some of the boys have experienced, do you want to risk giving off the wrong signal?

ANGIE: But I wasn't trying to send the wrong signal. Maybe I did though.

TONY: One part is to be sure about our intent, but then another part is even if our intent is good, how is it received?

ANGIE: So, are you saying, we shouldn't hug the kids and rub their backs?

TONY: No. I'm saying that we should do it with sensitivity to the meaning of our touch

RICARDO: What a crock. Look, if you know what you're doing go ahead. I hug the girls and the boys all the time. I'm not sure if I'd give them a backrub, but that's just me. If you're someone who is trying to sexually abuse these kids or send mixed messages you shouldn't be working here. Give Bill and Angie a little slack. They were just trying to do what felt right.

SHANTELL: I think it's wrong. I don't think we should be running around hugging and touching kids because it feels right. These kids are confused about touch and it's better to error on the side of caution and to avoid touch, except under some special circumstance. I hugged Andre when he left last week, but I wasn't running around hugging him when he was here. He knew I cared about him.

BILL: I don't touch simply because it feels right. I try to consider the meaning. All I was saying is, it's difficult to be sure about the message I'm sending, just like Tony said.

RICARDO: Look man, you did the right thing. I know Nikki. She is really a little kid inside looking for the affection she never got. If she took it sexually, I'd be surprised.

BILL But don't you think I should talk to her about it?

RICARDO: Sure, if that's your thing. Go ahead reassure yourself. Personally, I wouldn't be second guessing myself. If the kids get the wrong message at first they would know over time that I'm not like that. Most of them already do.

ANGIE: This boundary work is so difficult.

SHANTELL: Not if you're clear about your boundaries.

CAMILLE: Are you clear about them for yourself, or for what the kids need?

SHANTELL: Look, I know who I am, how close I want to be, and they read that in me. I don't violate their space, and they don't violate mine.

RICARDO: Except when they're angry.

CAMILLE (*Deflecting the direction of the conversation*): Strange you should use The word violate.

SHANTELL: Look Camille, don't try to analyze me.

TONY: Let's get back to Angie's comment. Shantell has expressed herself but I'd like to hear what some of the others think about boundaries.

RICARDO: It's like I said. If you respect your own boundaries and the kids' boundaries then its fine sometimes to get close and other times to create a little more space. It's like a little dance. You get a sense of when to move in and when to move away based on the music you hear.

BILL: That's insightful. I hadn't thought of it that way.

TONY: What way?

BILL: Boundaries are elastic, not rigid. We create them based on our understanding of what's going on and our feel for the music or the emotional tension or lack thereof that exists. In philosophy, we sometimes think of it as the existential hum, hum meaning something inside that calls us to truth in the moment.

RICARDO: Whoa, brother. You really took this to another place, but I think I like it.

SHANTELL: What's next on the agenda?

RICADRO (*Smiling*): What's the matter you afraid if we continue you might let down your guard?

SHANTELL: (*A piercing glance at Ricardo*).

RICARDO: Look, all I'm saying is that what matters is how you come across to the kids. You might read what I do differently than I do, and I might read what you do differently, but we can never fool the kids. They know if we are real, and sincere about intentions. If we're filled with self doubt, then they know.

ANGIE: But isn't a little self-doubt human?

RICARDO: Sure, but not about giving a backrub or hugging boys. If something inside you says, I'm not sure about what this means, then I'd say, don't do it.

BILL: But you sound so sensitive to your feelings now and what things means. How come you didn't sound that way when we were talking about gangs?

RICARDO: You misread me.

BILL: Well, I was thinking that there is something about you that comes across in a sincere way, especially when I see the kids huddled around you at in a conversation or activity. They seem to connect with you in a way they don't connect with me.

RICARDO: Maybe you're in your head too much? (*Ricardo's mood seems to change. He is more sympathetic now*). Like I said, man, it's not always what you say, but how you come across. I know their experience is different than mine, and I think they know that when I tell them I've been there (*Ricardo refers back to a conversation in Act I*). I just don't want and won't accept it becoming an excuse for them. Maybe I was wrong to let them stay up and watch the movie, but I think they know I wasn't trying to set anyone up or bribe them by letting down the rules a little. I've already talked to them about how they behaved and how disappointed I was.

TONY: Good.

RICARDO (*Continues as if making amends*): I was thinking, Shantell, that what you said earlier about culture was probably true in the sense that my culture is part of me, just as your dignity as a black woman defines you, and how you see things.

SHANTELL: How couldn't it!

RICARDO: It's just that I don't know how big a part. I know I'm not like a lot of my Hispanic friends, and you don't fit the stereotype of the warm, caring, black woman.

SHANTELL: What do you mean by that?

RICARDO: Well, as you said, you don't like to hug the kids. I see you much more like I might see a white business woman, dignified, well dressed and somewhat distant.

SHANTELL: I don't see myself as distant. I'm close to many of these kids. It's just that I think it is important to keep a little space between us because I know they will have to leave and I don't want to give them to get too attached.

BILL: I think Shantell provides a good role model. The girls and boys respect her for her commitment and professionalism. But I'm not sure how much culture is part of this. I know I rarely think about my culture or ethnicity.

RICARDO: That's because you're a white guy. But to me your whiteness is just as much a part of you as being Hispanic is part me.

BILL: What do you mean?

RICARDO: You act white. You have this sort of nondescript, bland way of fitting in.

BILL: I'm not non-descript, am I? I'm a little too heady maybe, but not non-descript?

SHANTELL: The reason you don't notice how people react to you is because of your skin color. You're seen as part of the establishment, rather than different. Whereas being black immediately influences what people see, being white evokes little response.

RICARDO (*Smiling, looking at Bill*): Look bro, I like you. I see you as unique, the philosopher who really cares about the kids. I was just trying to make a point, as Shantell just did, about how we are all seen differently.

ANGIE: How do you guys see me?

RICARDO: Raw, young, eager to do the right thing, caring.

BILL: I agree. I see you as a warm person trying to learn the ropes.

SHANTELL: Sometimes, I think you go a little overboard in trying to get the kids to like you.

ANGIE: But I care about, even love them, and I want to learn to feel the same way about me so they can care for others.

CAMILLE (*Has been observing and quiet until now*): That's a little risky. You don't want to mislead them by getting too attached. You won't be with them when they leave.

RICARDO: Maybe in spirit.

The conversation continues…

This play, which is based on conversations I participated in and listened to over a period of several years, first appeared in my column on www.cyc-net.org.

SELF IN ACTION

These are seven of my favorite sketches: The first sketch grew out of the reflection presented in the Introduction to this book:

FLYING BIRD NEST

I sit in my father's chair and stare at my feet, imagining my foot bones the way they appeared the in x-ray machine at the shoe store. My mother is in the kitchen checking the items in the grocery bags against the receipt. My older brother is out with his friends. My father is in the bathroom, the smell of his aftershave wafting over the classical music he plays on Saturday afternoons.

Here he comes. "I've got to get a haircut. I'll be right back, son. Then we can go and get those ice skates."

"I thought we were going now?"

"I'll only be about an hour."

"He's such a Jekyll and Hyde," my mother says to my aunt on the phone, talking about my father.

I look at the photos on the mantel of our family. They seem like pictures of someone else's family.

My father won't be back. He never comes right back when he goes for a haircut, but I keep hoping he will. While I wait, I go outside and shoot hoops. My brother and I put the basket and backboard on the roof so it hangs over the alley. One after another I chase down jump shots.

*

I walk up the hill at the treatment center surrounded by six boys. It's a nice fall day; geese fly overhead. Our feet slip slightly on the stones. I move closer to a couple boys who have a tendency to run away along the tracks on the other side of the hill. They seem okay.

"I hope we have hamburgers," Johnnie says.

"Yeah, me too," says Nick.

"Did you see the game last night?" Ron asks about the basketball game on TV.

"Yes," I say.

"I want to play pro ball some day," Bobby says.

I start to say, "Yyou better have some other options," then stop. It feels like a moment for dreaming.

We enter the double doors and begin to climb the stairs. The smell of hamburgers comes from the kitchen

We sit down around the small table. Groups of six and seven other boys are sitting around tables with their workers. We dig into the burgers and chips.

"I have a home visit this weekend," Alan, one of the boys, says.

"Your dad probably won't show," Tony, another youth responds.

"Asshole!" Alan reacts.

"Watch your language," I say, and "Tony stop jiving Alan."

"You workers never do what you say you're going to do," Joseph says quietly.

"What Joseph?" I ask.

"You never do what you say you're going to do."

"What do you mean?"

"You said you would find me a foster home so I could leave this dump."

"We've been trying."

"I know, you keep telling me that and that I'm ready to go, but I'm still waiting."

I pause, knowing that it might be a while before we can find foster parents who will take older boys, like the ones at our center.

Alan puts his thumb in Tony's burger. Tony backhands Alan across the top of the head.

"Knock it off!" I say...

*

I play until the sun gets low in the sky and the melted snow freezes and makes it too slippery to play, then go in for dinner. My mother makes bologna, beans, and fried potatoes for dinner. Afterwards, she knits, while I read about horses and my older brother makes a model airplane, cutting and gluing pieces of balsa wood to a tissue-paper pattern. Later he will bake the paper skin tight around the frame in the oven. In spring he will go into the attic, start it on fire, and throw it out the window for me to douse on the ground with the garden hose.

Before I go to bed, I do a flying bird nest on the gymnastic rings my brother and I made in the attic. Back and forth I swing inverted with my hands and legs behind me in the rings like a bird, over old photographs, appliances, and clothes in boxes...

*

(2006)...And after his periods of stasis, Foucault usually succeeded in achieving dramatic accelerations in his thinking and action. Thinking was action, and action was motion—and as a thinker and as a person Foucault chose to be in motion... To detach oneself from oneself—such a distance enables motion, and in turn, motion enables a recurrent activity of self detachment (Rabinow and Rose, The Essential Foucault, 1994, p. xxii).

WRITING YOUTH WORK: BRIAN AND ME

I wrote this sketch for my www.cyc-net.org column to describe the relationship between writing sketches and youth work:

As we interact with children and youth, we write child and youth care (a.k.a. youth work). Each moment and interaction becomes part of the evolving narrative of a meal, recreation activity, chore, or conversation, as well as, the youths' and our stories. We also write about child and youth care. Our stories, articles, and books, are put in print. Others read us, and what we have to say.

In this context, we are at our best when we show rather than tell. As protagonists (professional workers) and heroes (role models and mentors), we are human, trying to be present, open and available to mirror back our experiences of others. When we struggle and fail, we admit it and learn from our mistakes.

Our writing (dialogue, actions, and descriptions) looks, smells, and feels, like child and youth care. It isn't "scripted" or manipulated to serve some ulterior motive, modify behavior, or reach some outcome. Our voice comes and goes but always it is our voice that we want to speak in, not a voice that we think will please others.

The movement of our words and actions are, as Aristotle said about motion, the mode in which the present and future are one. We are with one another in the moment, immersed in our activity, disclosing trust as a way of being together as human beings.

Self informs us and makes us curious. This is what it's like for me, what's it like for you? We say or think, with the knowledge that the experiences of an interaction or moment are as diverse as the participants themselves.

As the material is worked and reworked in the mind and soul, an image or feeling is revealed in a new light. A moment for example, when a youth in a new situation, space or way asks, "Can I participate?" There is no clear beginning, plot, or ending, to these moments. Like images on film moving across a screen, each experience is a contribution to the montage we call, child and youth care.

Many years ago:

I am in an office at a residential treatment center, where I came to work a couple months ago, with several child and youth care workers from a previous treatment center that was closed. We brought along some of the boys who could not be placed elsewhere. I miss the old center. Things are different here.

Sitting across from me is Brian, a muscular sixteen year-old. It's about 7:45 a.m. We just finished breakfast and Brain is about to go to school. He's rubbing his hands together as he does almost constantly. I'm on guard. A couple days ago he broke the nose of one of the child and youth care workers I supervise.

I'm not sure I want to do this, but our team has decided that I should spend a few moments of one on one time with Brian everyday before school, to develop a relationship and help determine what triggers these aggressive outbursts. What makes it difficult is that it is seemingly impossible to predict when he will lash out. Things can be going fine and then suddenly he will take a swipe at you. The clinical social worker diagnosed him as "borderline psychotic." Through most of his childhood, his father beat him. Like many youth, he is torn between hating his father and loving him. Publicly, he often talks about his father as if he was a hero. We want to keep Brian here, but we're not sure if we can because of the danger he presents to the staff and other boys who are less disturbed.

I am sitting beyond arms length. It's an early spring day. Melted snow is dripping from the rain gutters above the window.

"I like Volkswagens," he says with a nervous laugh. His eyes flit around the room.

"Why?"

He grins, stops rubbing his hands, and leans forward slightly, "My dad had one once." He rocks back and forth in his chair. "Yeah, my dad had one."

Someone bangs on the door. I open it halfway. It's Juan. "Want to play cards?" he asks.

"I'm with Brian right now."

"Why does he get all the attention? I think I'll bust someone's nose then I can get one on one every morning."

"Shut up Juan!" Brian says.

"I have some time after school during your free time. We can play cards then." I tell Juan.

"Okay, see you later."

He puts his foot in the door so I can't close it, laughs and runs off. Brian is standing by the window, watching the drops of water and talking to himself.

"He wouldn't let me ride in the Volkswagen."

"Why not?" I ask.

"He said I had to be good, but I never was."

"What would you think if we worked on a model car tomorrow?" I ask.

He puts his head down, makes a few funny noises, and puts his face a few inches from mine. "I want to make a Mustang."

"I thought you liked Volkswagens?" I take a step back.

"You're afraid of me, aren't you?" he says.

"I'm afraid you might hit me, and I want to be sure that you don't."

"I could if I wanted to."

"Do you want to?"

He laughs nervously and fakes a left jab. "Volkswagens are too slow. I hate them." He pauses, then says, "I hate you."

"Why?"

"Because you think you're my dad."

I start to say why do you think that, but catch myself and wait for him to continue.

"You think you're my dad because you want to make a Volkswagen," he repeats and walks out.

88

"See you tomorrow," I say and take a deep breath.

The next day Brian arrives a few minutes early. It's turned cloudy and cold again. I have the model car kit and some glue on newspaper on top of the desk.
"Did you get a Mustang?"
"Yes," we sit on the sides of a corner of the desk. It strikes me that some of these parts could be turned into weapons.
He giggles and flicks a finger at me.
"Show me how to make it." I say.
He jokingly sniffs the glue.
I frown.
"What?" he says and starts to glue to parts together. "Watch what I do."
"I will."
For a moment, his hands seem steady.
I relax, let down my guard.

...and the picture evolves.

CLASS

I'm sitting in a circle in a large room with fourteen students in my class, four youth, and a youth worker, who is a member of our research group who invited our class to the shelter for youth where he works. A few minutes ago, he took us on a tour. Then we walked here, to the administration building, to discuss what we saw and learned.
One of the youth is telling us about the shelter, his history in foster care and his goals in life. It seems like a speech he has given many times. I'm a little uneasy about how much personal information he's sharing in front of strangers, but the youth worker is letting him go. At one point the youth talks about how he's learned to play the system, and I wonder if he isn't playing us. His fast talk and nervous, cocky body language tell me something is still very unsettled in him.
Then he says something like, "My foster mother wants me to pay for a pair of pants. I ain't payin' for no pair of pants. She gets money for that every month. Why should I pay?" He looks across the room at me. "Professor, I want to know what you think. Is that right? Should she make me pay? "
I begin to contemplate what to say. I learned long ago not to let myself be set up as an expert, but I still feel uneasy about in being in this position. Before I can answer, the youth is distracted by a comment from someone else and shifts to another part of the room. As the conversation continues, I wonder what I would have said. Maybe I would have questioned him further to see whether or not he didn't have his own answer? It's always better when they can discover what to do on their own. Or, I might have said, "I'm not sure, I think I'd have to know more, but in general I think it is good to start paying something for your own things as you get older, especially if they are extra items that go beyond what foster parents

are paid to provide." But this might have only led to more resistance by allowing him to disagree with something that he didn't want to do, but deep down knew he should. He would have no choice in that public setting but to save face, even if he knew what I said was right.

On my way to my car afterwards, I think about how, even after years of study and practice, I am still uneasy and uncertain in these situations, and how understanding these moments is an important part of the work and my life. A gift. Next week I'll talk about this with my class. If I can, I'll also try to follow up with the youth worker and youth to get their interpretations of what was happening.

TOUCH

Kent approaches Cottage Four with two bags of groceries for Cindy's going away party. It's a nice spring afternoon. Children are playing in the courtyard circled by the cottages. Six girls who are playing volleyball across the way run toward him. By the time he gets out his key, Maria, 14, has stepped in front of him and blocked the door.

"Move out of the way, please, Maria."

"Make me," she says.

"Just step aside."

"Yeah, get out of the way, you tramp," Nicole says.

Maria, who loves a crowd, stands firm. Kent sets down the grocery bags, and asks her again. She moves slightly aside until Kent picks up the bags then jumps back in front of the door. Kent sets down the bags again, grabs her by the shoulders and gently moves her to the side. "Now, please, stay there."

Maria smiles, then just as Kent turns to get the grocery bags again, she pulls him into her and falls with Kent on top into the railing next to the door. "Look, he's raping me! He's raping me!" *She shouts loud enough for everyone to hear.*

"He is. He's raping her," *Kelly says and the other girls giggle.*

Meanwhile, Kent tries to back away but Maria quickly wraps her legs around him.

"What's going on here?" *asks Ms Marley, the assistant director and lead therapist, as she approaches from the administration building.*

Maria releases her grip.

"Kent's raping Maria," *Ellen, another one of the girls says.*

Standing and facing Ms Marley, Kent says, "Maria, obviously, is being very uncooperative. I was trying to take these groceries inside and she blocked the door. When I moved her to the side, she pulled me on top of her."

"I did not. He was raping me," *Maria says.*

"Go inside, Maria!" *Ms Marley says.*

"But it wasn't my fault."

"Go inside!"

"I won't bitch!"

90

"Well then, we'll just have to examine your privileges, I guess," Marley says.

"You're always taking away my privileges," Maria says, and reluctantly goes inside. Ms Marley has the final say over all privileges, such as when the girls and boys at the center can go off grounds or on home visits alone on the bus.

"Kent, could we speak after the party?" Marley asks.

"Sure."

At one point during the party, Kent stands to the side of the punch bowl with co-workers Nancy and Debbie. Two girls are dancing near the stereo speakers; the rest are circled around Cindy looking at her going away gifts. After the party she will leave with her new foster parents who have yet to arrive.

"Don't worry about Marley. She won't do anything, other than caution you," Debbie says.

"Oh, it's not her I'm worried about. It's the general attitude. There is such a double standard."

"What do you mean?" Nancy asks.

"People are so uptight about a man working with and having contact with girls. At the treatment center I worked at for boys, no one got up tight if one of the women hugged them or even helped them with showers. Here, a man is guilty until proven otherwise."

"Yes,, unfortunately, I'm afraid that's true. But we know you didn't do anything. Maria is always pulling that stuff, using the abuse card."

"Guilty until innocent," Kent sighs and walks over to say goodbye to Cindy.

After the party Kent walks across to Marley's office. She's working late as always. She's been at the center 25 years and is a knowledgeable and experienced therapist. The door is open.

"Kent, come in." She stands from her desk and motions for Kent to sit in an armchair across from her desk chair, then folding her skirt under her, she sits down. "I just wanted to chat a little bit about the incident with Maria."

"Yeah, she really set me up for that."

Marley offers a consoling smile and waits for Kent to continue. When he doesn't, she says, "You know of course how sensitive these things can be?"

"Are you saying it was intentional?"

"Oh no, by no means. What I'm saying is that we have to be aware of how the girls interpret physical contact."

"Do you think I gave Maria the wrong message?"

"I really don't know what transpired. I came in at the end of the incident. I'm not blaming anyone."

"The answer is no. On the other hand if you are asking if I am turned on by some of the girls, the answer is yes. Any normal man would be, just as the women who work here are turned on by some of the boys, but no normal person would act in any way on those feelings....Besides that's not the reason why everyone gets so concerned anyways."

"What is?" Marley asks, surprised by his anger.

"Lawsuits. Investigations. You're afraid Maria might tell her parents or file a complaint and it will get out in the public. Everyone is afraid. So am I. We might as well have robots working in this place."

"I won't deny that we worry about this, but I assure you that that is not the reason I invited you here...I simply thought it would be helpful to talk about it. I am aware of Maria's history and her tricks to get attention, and I think you are too, and a very good worker, but I thought it would be helpful to talk. These are very difficult issues for all of us."

"Yes, especially for men working with girls."

"Oh, I agree. Unfortunately, these unfair stereotypes interfere with our ability to find and keep men who sincerely want to help, and there is nothing these girls need more than a secure, caring adult male. That's why you are so valuable to us."

Relieved Kent talks with Marley for a while. It feels good to be able to talk openly and Marley seems very understanding.

*When he returns to the cottage, the girls **are finishing** the party dishes. As he pitches in and talks with Cindy about her future **plans**, Maria walks by and brushes against him, her seductive look out of place **with** her childlike face. Kent ignores her.*

*Later that night, before bedtime, Kent reads **a** story to the girls. He is a good reader. Despite complaints about having to turn off the TV, most of the girls enjoy ending the day this way, especially when he is the reader. As he reads two girls sit on the floor with their backs to the couch next to his legs. One sits on the armrest and looks down at the book, while one girl sits beside him. Maria is standing off to the side, next to the plants.*

About five minutes into the reading, he feels a head on his shoulder on the side of the couch where no one had been sitting. The other girls giggle. Maria is cuddled against him, the way a child would cuddle up against a parent. Kent tenses. A friend, a male worker at another center, was accused of sexual abuse when he sat next to two girls in running shorts.

Maria raises her head and says. "Keep reading."

"Yeah, I want to hear the end," Nicole says.

Kent goes on with the story. Maria puts her head back on his shoulder.

THE ALLEY (A SKETCH FROM MY YOUTH-- BEFORE FRAGMENTATION)

(1954) I kick the ball above the garage roof. On the way down, it hits the edge of the rain gutter, falls on the ground, and hisses, punctured on a rusty piece of metal. I go inside. Our flat is on the first floor. We live on Milwaukee's Northwest side. No one is home. My mother is at the grade school where she's the principal's secretary. My father is at the Northwestern Mutual Life Insurance Company where he's worked since he was a young man.

I won the ball at Summer Fun Club for most pushups, 28. It's about the size of a basketball, only the rubber is thinner and the seams go out, like my ribs, instead of in. I put tape on the puncture and pump it up. It still leaks. Red will fix it. I walk down the alley, dodging horse apples from the garbage wagons. Despite the shit, I prefer the alley. It's shorter.

Like most neighborhoods around here, ours has little shops and parks within walking distance, and clapboard duplexes on elm lined streets that look pretty much the same after a while. One day I entered the house to my right and saw my friend Claudia's mother vacuuming with no bra, her tits, like hoses, hanging down to her panties. Pretty disgusting.

I close my eyes and count my steps, trying to make it to the end of the alley without looking. I almost make it to the end before I open my eyes. Tires are behind the station. Sometimes I hide here in games of "can." Red is under a Plymouth. He sees my shoes, slides out, his face covered with grease.

"What can I do for you Matt?" he asks.

I show him the ball.

"Flat, uh."

"Yup."

"Easy enough to fix."

"I thought so."

The bell rings. Red goes out to pump gas. A Plymouth is on the rack. I sit in the old shoeshine chair in the office and look out the window. Emil Horn's Drug Store is across the street. Just beyond that is Freedman's grocery store, where we have a tab.

"This will just take a second," Red says after he puts the money in the cash register. He scrapes the spot around the leak with a file, spreads the glue evenly, puts a patch on top, and smoothes out the edges. Then he pumps it up. "There, that ought to do it," he tosses it to me.

"Thanks, Red. How much?"

"No charge."

"I owe you," I say, like my dad says sometimes.

"Sure."

I walk to Wally's restaurant, which is on the other side of the alley, just past the barbershop, and sit at the lunch counter.

"Pumpkin seeds," I put three cents on the counter.

"You sure like your salt," Wally, the owner, a friendly old guy, says. "How's your mother?"

"Fine."

"You be good to her."

"I will."

"Here," he gives me a penny red licorice for free.

"Thanks."

On the way home, in between bites of licorice, I chew pumpkin seed shells around the edges, while I bounce the ball with the other hand. They last longer that way. When I get home, I gulp down a glass of water, and comb my duck's tail. Then I lie perfectly still on my bed.

93

The cracks in the ceiling are the Amazon River. My cat, Rocky, jumps up on the bed. I pet him. He purrs, rolls on his back so I can scratch his stomach. It's dead silent, like nothing. The front door opens. Rocky jumps off the bed, meows. It's my mother. She feeds him regularly. I do it when I feel like it.

"Hi Matt." She's exhausted. In two weeks school starts again. She's the principal's secretary. They're getting ready. I like the way she looks. She's wearing a skirt and short-sleeved blouse.

"What's for dinner?" I ask.

"I thought I'd make sweetbreads, boiled potatoes, and beans."

"Can we have fried potatoes?"

"Yes, I guess so," she sighs. "Why don't you go and wait for your father."

She wants me out of her hair. I ride my bike to the bus stop, three blocks away on Sherman Boulevard. A bus stops. The door opens with a hiss, like the hiss from the punctured ball. He's not on this one. Another passes without stopping. Last week, I waited until it was dark--one hiss after another with no sign of him. It was as if day faded with each gasp of air. Pretty soon it was dark.

I can see him on the next one before it stops. He's standing, ready to get off, newspaper under his arm. He looks cool with his dark hair is slicked back and his dark blue suit, white shirt and dark blue and white polka-dot tie.

"Hi son," he says, his voice drownded out by the motor.

I walk by his side with my bike.

"How was your day?" he asks.

I tell him about the ball.

"That Red is something else, isn't he?"

"Yes, how was your day?"

"Oh, let's just say uneventful."

Our house is fourth from this end of the alley, the end opposite the gas station.

"Hi Bill," my mother says, turning from the stove.

"Hi Marie." He takes off his coat and sits in his chair in the living room with the newspaper. My older brother comes home from football practice. He's in junior high school; I start next year.

"Let's eat," my brother says.

"In a few minutes," say mother.

My older brother washes up. "So, what are we having?" my father walks in the kitchen.

"Sweetbreads."

"Harry called today, he's coming in for the convention," my father says about my uncle who lives in New York and will be coming to the home company where he used to work with my father, before he got a branch office in the Big Apple. He wears wild ties and Lady Godiva suspenders and tells corny jokes. My mother tells about her day at the school. I go into the attic and swing on the gymnastic rings my brother and I hung from the rafters.

At dinner, my brother tells about his job cutting grass and practicing football. I don't say much, I never do unless I want to get a reaction, like the time I told my mother I was glad when my grandmother died.

"I'm going up to see Ralph," my father says after dinner and goes upstairs where the Barry's live. Mr. Barry wears a suit too. He travels for another company. Mrs. Barry works in an office like my mom for the government, not a school, highways, I think. They don't have kids.

I put on my khaki pants with the big side pockets and powder blue jersey and walk down the alley to the park that is only a couple blocks away, and field balls during batting practice before the softball game. They let us do it. All the kids in the neighborhood participate. We chase down the balls they hit. The one who gets the most points for the summer wins--5 points for a fly ball with no glove, 3 with a glove, 2 for a one-bouncer (glove or no glove) and 1 for a grounder. There's no prize or anything, just winning, whatever that's worth.

I get seven balls, 19 points--total for the season, 742. Arbiture has 840. I'll never catch him. Russo shows up. We walk around looking for girls. He has a brush haircut. Maybe I'll get one. No, I like my duck's tail. Kathy and Mary, who we see almost every time we come, approach. Last week, Russo got bare tit from Mary, in the bushes, behind the pavilion. He's ahead of me on that. When Mary and Russo go off to the bushes again, I'm left with Kathy. I don't like her.

"See you, I've got to go home" I say, and leave.

It's dark. Wally's is closed, but Red's is still open. Kent is working. He has a tattoo from the navy and wants to go to Michigan State to study forestry on the G.I. Bill. I wave; he waves back as I enter the alley. It's private here at night, away from traffic, and people. I walk slowly trying not to get shit on my shoes.

I swing on the gate; it creaks. My mom's watching TV. I hate it when she knows I'm coming. My dad and Mr. Barry are upstairs, drinking cocktails and reciting Jabberwoke. I sit on the back steps and listen:

"Twas brillig, and the slithy toves
  Did gyre and gimble in the wabe:
All mimsy were the borogroves,
  And the mome raths outgrabe...."

Mr Barry says and my father goes:

"Beware the Jabberwock, my son!
  The jaws that bite, the claws that catch!
Beware the Jubjub bird, and shun
  The fruminous Bandersnatch!"

I can imagine how stupid they look: two grown men all dressed up, drunk and speaking nonsense. My father gets really weird sometimes. "A real Jekyll or Hyde," my mom says. I throw my clothes down the shoot and go to my room. The moon is out. My fort, a refrigerator box, with a rug on the floor, is under the window. It's not a real fort like the one I make when we go up north in the summer. I can't wait to go. Then, when we get there, I worry about it ending. Sometimes it rains. I don't want to think about it.

95

I can't see the Amazon River. I can see the ball though. It's on the window ledge, ribs sticking out like my ribs. Wonder if Russo got bare tit? I'll get some pretty soon. Maybe Kathy will give it to me, even though I don't like her? School starts in a few days. The moon dips behind the garage. It's pitch dark. I lay perfectly still. There's nothing.

THE VISIT

(1997) A pick-up truck with a man sitting inside is parked in the driveway.
"Hello," his voice is deep, his complexion tanned or perhaps wind-burned.
"Daniel?"
"Yes."
It's been more than twenty-five years since he ran away from the treatment center.
"Come inside."
I give him a cold drink. He walks around the house with it in his hands looking at the paintings. "Where is she?"
"At her studio in New Mexico, painting."
"Your son?"
"Grown."

(1988) "Nothing is real," Devon wrote, quoting John Lennon at the beginning of his paper on parallel universes.
"Why didn't you turn it in? It's really good," I say, holding the paper I just un-crumpled from the ball I found in the bottom of his backpack, after getting a call from his teacher about his missing paper.
"I must have forgot."
"How could you forget?"
"I don't know."
I look at him. We sit down and talk. "Tell me about how we can exist in two places at the same time," I say.

(1997) Daniel and I sit down in the kitchen.
"What brings you back?" I ask.
"Not sure."
"Have you been dancing?"
"No."
He walks into the living room and stares through the enclosed porch to the street.
"I was going for a run, want to come along?" I ask.
"Yes."
The air is clear, crisp. We run north along the shore, a route we took many times when he was at the treatment center. As we move together over the sidewalks, it's as if time stood still.

Daniel rents an apartment, gets a road construction job, and tries, at age 42, to return to dancing, long past the age when his body will let him do it well. We run together two or three times a week. One night, I stop by the dance studio. He walks over with a towel on his shoulders. The scars on his body from his abuse seem more pronounced.

"How long you been here?" he asks.

"Just a few minutes."

We have coffee in a small shop next to the studio. It's raining, a cold November rain.

"I saw my parents."

"How are they?"

"The same."

"Carla and your son?"

"I couldn't find them."

Later, when I drop him off in front of his apartment above the hardware store, he says, "I'm not sure how long I'll stay. Will you come to see me perform?"

"Yes."

The performance is held in an Eastside loft. Several students sit with me on folding chairs, as Daniel takes the stage and moves to composer John Adam's aching harmonies. It's an acrobatic, if not graceful, performance. His steps are bold, strong with pain, anger, and relief, but not as intense or free as his recital when he was younger and we had enrolled him in modern dance classes.

"I wish I could dance like that," a young woman female student, says outside, her face naked, innocent.

"He's gone," the landlord says a few days later when I go to pick him up for a run.

"Did he say where?"

"No, he just paid his rent and left."

(1997)An old woman, made up like a small girl, leaves the coffee shop. "Good bye, honey," she says on her way out the door. I'm sitting next to the window working on a sketch.

Meanwhile, the regulars sitting at the counter continue to talk about the news. More cuts--cuts for the poor, cuts for the sick, cuts for the neighborhood, cuts for the factory workers. "There are no more decent paying jobs," one of them says.

"Go into computers, that's where the money is," a younger man says.

"I'm too old."

"Can't teach an old dog new tricks, huh?"

"Something like that, I guess."

A middle-aged man with a cast on his foot and a book enters, sits down next to a man in a business suit, who sells industrial real estate.

"You ought to take a look at this." The real estate man hands a piece of paper to the other man. "It's a perfect space for what you're looking for."

"When my foot heals," the man with the cast on his foot says.

"What are you reading?"

"Samuel Beckett."

"Waiting for Godot, right?"

As I write about Daniel, my pen scratches on paper, then a pause, while in the margins I continue my search for character.

A sparrow flies into the window above my head, falls to the ground, flutters, and dies. People rush in, and out, unaware of what happened. The sun rises above the houses across the street and falls on my shoulder. A crow appears in a tree, its eyes darting about. The sparrow's feathers flitter in a gentle breeze; the crow waits. A woman enters, orders her coffee, stands to the side, like the crow, and looks around.

"Light?" the man with the cast on his foot asks.

"From the north."

"How much?"

"We can work something out."

"No, I meant how much light?"

"Oh, plenty..."

The young woman catches my eye as she leaves. "No one likes to be judged, least of all you," someone told me once, not in so many words, but in words that meant the same thing.

I look at the dead bird again. "Sputzi's. Wwe used to shoot them with a sling shot and cook them on a stick," my father used to say.

"I've got to go," the man with the cast says.

"When you get a chance, take a look at it. I think it will be an excellent space for you to show your photographs."

There is a good shot right here, a dead sparrow and a crow, I consider telling the man, but don't--this is my scene. Men and women in business suits walk past, feet too light to stick in Wheat Fields With Crows. Outside the door, the man sees the bird, nudges it with his cane and moves down the street. The crow watches and waits until there is a pause in the movement of people, then swoops down, claws its prey, and flies away.

The show over, I put aside my work and grade papers. The students have written stories about their experiences with youth, much the way I have written these stories. Some are very moving. Next week they will begin juxtaposing sketches from their childhoods. I read their stories for about an hour more, then, as I stand to gather my things, I look at the smudge above my head, wondering what the bird saw last, its reflection or the blue sky or a bright light?

"Don't forget your gloves," my mother used to say

GRAFFITI ART

About three years after my class took the tour with Carlos (see The Tour in Chapter Four), I go with a new class to community meeting at the center where Carlos has become the executive director for a community meeting. The topic is graffiti art. People are coming together to see if they can stop the kids from tagging their garage doors and houses. With the rise of Hip Hop music, graffiti art has grown in popularity. This has the neighbors, who can't tell the difference between graffiti art and gang art, worried. Both forms of tagging make them worry. Besides, whether its gang or graffiti art no one wants it on their property, except some of the shop owners who give permission as a marketing tool to draw kids in to buy a skateboard or CD, DVD game, or T shirt. A panel with a judge, an art professor, an elected official, a youth, a graffiti artist, a skateboard shop owner, a neighbor, and the leader of the city's graffiti art clean up crew has been formed. A cocky youth from the center is the moderator.

"This is my court, judge," a young man dressed in "hip hop" clothes looks down the panel at the judge who has just interrupted him. The judge and audience laugh. I'm sitting with the students about ten rows back. The room is packed.

"Young people need to have an opportunity to express themselves," the art professor says.

"Yes, not all graffiti is bad. There is graffiti art and gang art. Graffiti art is an expression of Hip Hop culture," the skateboard shop owner says.

"Kids will always express themselves in their way," the renowned graffiti artist says.

"Yes, but they have no right to do it on someone else's property," a city official who responds to graffiti complaints says.

"Older people can discriminate between gang art and graffiti art. It all scares them when they see it in the neighborhood," an elected official says and the neighbor nods agreement.

My mind drifts to a poem I am working on:

Weave and Bop; Dip and Slide

Weave and bop;
dip and slide

Weave and bop;
dip and slide

     What's up, man?
     What's happening, brother

     press flesh
     wanna *be*

CHAPTER 6

Weave and bop;
dip and slide

      break   dance
      spin on your head
      force time
      to stand still

Weave and bop;
dip and slide

      ride blue lights
      and bass speakers
      roam

Weave and bop;
dip and slide

      dwell like a man
      inside a woman
      he does not love
      in a reservation of despair

Weave and bop;
dip and slide

      match colors
      this gang; that gang
      walk your baby to the store
      this hood; that hood
      find a morsel of sweetness
      for a tiny mouth
      your mouth; my mouth

Weave and bop;
dip and slide

Weave and bop;
dip and slide

      wanna   *be*

"Well why don't we create spaces where youth can paint their graffiti art. The center here has devoted the walls of the garage to graffiti art," the skateboard shop owner says, pointing to the back of the room and the doorway to a large garage attached to the center, which is in an old factory.

"This will solve part of the problem, but young people will always tag places owned by other people, especially if the youth feel disenfranchised. Once you become a property owner your attitude changes, but most of these kid's families can't afford their own property," the renowned artist says.

"Studies suggest that providing legal public spaces alone doesn't necessarily work," the judge says.

"Does putting young people in jail as felon's work?" the skateboard owner says.

"I think we need a two-pronged, approach. Tough laws and opportunities for legal expression," the elected official says.

"Look at all the space devoted to ads and billboards selling these kids things they don't need. They invade most of our public spaces," the skateboard owner says.

"Yes, but the owners of these ads pay for the space they use," the elected official responds.

"Well then that's the problem, isn't it? Young people in our community can't afford the space to express themselves," the cocky moderator replies.

"We could probably provide all the space they needed and still have illegal graffiti. That's part of the process; tagging spaces that are illegal. Kids have done it for generations and they will do it for generations in the future. It's part of the nature of adolescence. I did it until I bought my own property," the renowned artist says.

"So what's the solution?" the facilitator asks.

"To get our society to value art in all its forms," the art professor responds...

Based on the applause and comments, it becomes obvious that the panel and audience is stacked in favor of graffiti artists. The judge, elected official, and graffiti enforcer are trying to be rational with an audience that is convinced that cracking down on graffiti is just another way to crack down on youth.

As the discussion continues I look around the packed room. Teenage mothers are clustered to the right of the stage with their babies on their hips, a few youth are making noise in the back of the room, seemingly disinterested in the conversation, people in the audience are nodding their heads, most in support of the value of graffiti art as a means of expression for youth people. We viewed the art in the garage before the discussion. I was very impressed with the talent, but like the neighbor on the panel has said earlier, I wouldn't want it on my garage without my permission. The evening ends without resolution. Everyone on the panel feels it was a good dialogue.

As the students and I part, I say, "Lets talk about this next week," then go directly home, stopping on the way for an ice cream cone. There is no graffiti art in my neighborhood. We all own our homes. For the most part it's a good accepting, diverse, open neighborhood, but tonight it feels like something is missing, perhaps the sense of community that goes with trying to solve a real problem that affects the lives of everyone in the neighborhood.

A few days later, three young adults are arrested for "tagging" the Milwaukee Art Museum, a brand new building designed by a famous architect. It makes the main pages of the newspapers whereas most graffiti crimes get no attention. Members of the public are angry. They want to give longer jail sentences to youth who deface their buildings. The anger is understandable, but the solution, like many reactive policies and solutions. There is no mention of the discussion we had at the youth center.

"So what do you think," I ask my class the following week.

"Like you said earlier, one of the toughest things youth workers have to do is say no and validate at the same time. Graffiti art on garages is not acceptable, but graffiti art is," an astute young man says.

"Did they do that at the meeting?"

"No," a young woman says.

"What do you mean?" another student asks.

"The tone of the meeting seemed to suggest that most of the panel members and audience were giving permission by not saying no strongly enough to painting graffiti on garages."

"Yeah, their anger against politicians and the system seemed to make them relinquish their personal authority or will to stop the problem and create new opportunities for the youth to express themselves..."

"I should have said something," I say.

"Yeah, me too..."

CHAPTER 7

MOTION, STILLNESS, WAITING, ANTICIPATING...

Themes like motion, stillness, waiting, anticipating, space, place, light and dark have been undercurrents in my sketches. In preparation for a workshop at the University of Victoria School of Child and Youth Care, I mused on these and other themes as written below, and then presented my thoughts to a group of students, faculty, and community members who shared their own ideas and examples of how the themes resonated with their experiences.

Muse: To consider thoughtfully, or at length, ponder...

MOTION AND STILLNESS

As a youth and youth worker, I was constantly in motion. I was moving, doing something. Motion was always there at the edge of my consciousness--something I did, heard, and/or flowed between us, that I could not quite understand, yet vital to knowing my experience and the experience of others. The titles of my novels were *In Motion* and, *Floating,* because this emphasized the meaning and importance of motion in work with youth.

Sometimes, I think of motion as the existential hum or a rumble beneath the surface that we often feel and hear, a life force perhaps? Motion is also, as Aristotle said, the mode in which the future and present are one (cited in Nabokov, 1981, p.27), or perhaps a state in which we can be totally in the moment. And, then, motion is just plain movement, or getting from here to there or nowhere; the movement without which it is impossible to act or imagine being alive.

Motion, action and thinking are connected in some way. To Foucault, thinking was action, and action was motion (Rabinow and Rose, *The Essential Foucault,* 1994, p. xxii). I run everyday because I enjoy moving. I do some of my best thinking. My mind seems to clear, and open to creative writing and problem solving.

Frequently, after the initial pain subsides and the endorphins kick in, I get the runners high. My activity and I are one. Time is lost and everything is in synch. I can go for several blocks and not remember the distance in between. It is my flow, or optimal experience (Csikszentmihalyi, 1990), and an example of how struggle in life leads to fulfillment.

Similarly, in youth work, I felt most at one with what I was doing when I was moving or doing something. We would run together, or sit quietly talking, or engage in some sort of physical struggle. "You have to like to move around, act, be engaged," I tell my youth work students. "Knowing how to move and where to be in relationship to the youth is a major skill in the work." Then I go into comparisons with modern dance, basketball, jazz, hockey, and other metaphors, that help show how our movements and positions influence the outcomes of our interactions.

Rhythm *&* *Motion* *connected*

Rhythm, motion, and stillness are closely related--the rhythms of our motions, perhaps as we seek resolution/stillness. Rhythmic interactions forge human connections (Maier, 1992), and let us know when a struggle is ending--the tension in the arms, back, and neck eases and subsides. As in modern dance, we line up and pass through, close or far. Boundaries and human connections are formed by our positioning, mirroring back, by our pauses, and ability to freeze ourselves in the timelessness of a moment. We are in and out of synch with youth and their developmental rhythms.

When I feel connected to others, motion is usually involved--for example, the shared rhythm of a conversation. We are doing something *with* each other: talking, working walking, dance, or running. I was often connected to the troubled boys when we were running, swimming, or playing one-on-one basketball. For example, I used to get a small group of them up early in the morning for a run. At first the pain made it difficult. Then as they got in shape, often we experienced a feeling of harmony in the middle of the run when we shared a common pace.

As a child I was always in motion. I felt a need to move. I ran from or to something. The murmur and hum always seemed to be there, just beneath the surface. Moving made me feel free, at least for the moment. I often moved from one place or thing to another, one dream or fantasy to another, childhood to youth to adulthood and back. Usually this went smoothly, but sometimes I did not want something to change or end, so I moved away, or avoided the transition. I went somewhere else, or did not show up, or I sped up the transition by moving ahead or away from what I was doing.

Many of the boys I worked with stayed in constant motion. They ran to or from somewhere or nowhere to keep busy, as thoughts and feelings raced through and riddled their bodies and minds. They did not want to put their heads on their pillows at night and be alone with these thoughts and feelings. They ran up and down the halls, onto the streets, into the woods, or walked away from our activity, because they could not wait to fail again. They were not used to smooth transitions. Things usually went badly when they moved from one place or activity to another. Their histories of movement and transition had been filled with failure and rejection. They had moved from one home to another, from awake to asleep, asleep to awake, and from crafts to dinner with some difficulty and fear. They did not have a normal sense of moving from one thing or place to another with relative ease and success, much less with moving from one challenging event to another. Learning to experience and master transitions was a big part of their care. Getting from here to there successfully, without rejection, fights, abuse, failure or neglect helped them deal with change and separation.

I am often most present, or open and available, when I am moving. Like the actor Wilhem Defoe said in his Inside the Actor's Studio interview on TV, "I am out of my head and into my body when I am in motion (acting)."

"I continue lost in the rhythm of my gait," I write in the opening scene to my self-portrait. Or, as Simon Ortiz suggests in his poem about presence, I am comfortable with the space that is myself (Ortiz, 1992, p. 126). Sex and motion, of course, are inextricably linked. We move to please others and ourselves.

There is smooth, jerky, continuous, and discontinuous, in and out of synch motion, each showing and telling something about an interaction or experience. Knowing these movements and motions and their relationship to what characters are thinking, feeling etc. is a major part of sketching as well as other forms of understanding lives and human interactions. It is body language. Watching others move their hands, feet, eyes, body, etc., tells us what they mean if we know how to look.

On the other hand, I am often moving toward stillness. I move to find peace and quiet, or am drawn to moving toward a place of quiet and stillness, such as the peace I find when I am exhausted after a run. I long to just be, or to search for just-so-ness, or I am moving toward death, or to return to the womb. I like to be in a still place, empty of thought and worry, a place I find I spend too little time. In the middle of a run I loose all contact, sometimes, with time and space. I am suspended, still, yet moving, just being.

As a boy, I stared at my feet, or the wall until there was nothing. When I hurt inside, I felt better just being totally still, or numb. I stiffened my body on my bed until nothing moved. It was one way I had of coping.

Youth, I think, often run-around, make noise, holler, and move to achieve similar states. They hear and try to rid themselves of the hum or rumble. Something moves inside them and they move to get away from it. Their anxiety is uncontrollable except when they run, fight, or lash out. Motion is a defense against the pain inside. Stillness is a dream, to be in a state of nothing, their heads and bodies rid of the thoughts and call to action that drive them to move and act the way they do. As a young boy, my mother used to get concerned when I ran and hollered through the house for no apparent reason.

In a sketch in my self-portrait, I am seeking, searching, running in place, always between and in states of light and dark, two themes, which will be discussed in a moment. In this context, motion was first a precursor, and later a tool, for using self to understand boys who ran and hollered to rid themselves of despicable thoughts and fears beyond my imagination (a longing for a sense of stillness and just being beyond anything I had experienced).

Like an Edward Hopper painting, my scenes are moving and still (Strand, 2001, p. 4). They are glimpsed in passing, still lives captured on my canvas as I move by. I am compelled to stay and leave, wait and anticipate, linger and move on. These are the rhythms of lives. Not always in synch or out of synch, but both, the in and out of synch-ness of how we seek resolution, the yin and yang of the constant move toward meaning, or purpose, the never ending journey, here, compelled to stay and leave.

WAITING AND ANTICIPATING

Much of youth is about waiting. I waited for someone to show up, to go someplace, or for something to happen. Sometimes I tried to make things happen; other times I just "hung out" waiting for things to happen. I would dream about and plan out the things I wanted to happen: a vacation up north, a trip someplace, a date, sex. Time passed so slowly when I waited for these things. I tired of waiting, stopped waiting and tried to make them happen sooner, which never seemed to work. Sometimes, I counted the hours thinking that would move things faster. It never did. I waited in the dentist's office or for my father to come home on the bus. I wanted him to come, but sometimes he didn't. I didn't want my turn with the dentist to come, but it always did. In the Army Reserves I hurried up and waited. I waited to be an adult, to drive, to grow a mustache, for the "one," the girl who didn't come, but whom I finally met when I wasn't waiting. (Often the things that meant the most in my youth were not the things I waited for.) I waited at the new shopping mall: I waited bored out of my skull; I waited, waited, waited.

In Samuel Beckett's famous play, *Waiting for Godot*, two men Estragon and Vladamir are waiting for someone named Godot, maybe to save them, maybe not. We do not know this person, or what he represents, or what he stands for. Much speculation has been made about the meaning of the play. But in the end, these are probably just two men waiting, and that's the theme of the play, as it is a theme in life.

The boys I worked with seemed to be constantly waiting, mainly for something to happen, mainly something good, I think. They had waited in fear, based on a history of the things they waited for never really happening, while something they weren't waiting for did: rejection, abuse, the police, a slap across the face, sexual abuse, and failure. Yet, they still waited and believed something good would happen. They would be saved, cared for, liked, admired, or famous, despite the odds against it. Daniel, the boy in several sketches who is a composite of two boys I knew, waited, wondering if he would be like his father, while he waited for the chance to dance and show others his creativity. He tested and waited for me to hurt him. It took all my strength not to do what he was waiting for. His sense of waiting changed, slightly.

Like I waited for my father at the bus stop to show up after work, they waited for their parents who never showed up, while my father always did, later sometimes, but he always came home. My mother was always there when she was supposed to be. I did not have to wait for her. Their mothers were rarely there when they were supposed to be. Yet they waited for them to "show up." Even when their parents were there they waited for them to show up. Physically present their parents were often elsewhere, drunk, drugged, preoccupied, self absorbed, unavailable. The youth waited to be in their presence but no one was home. They were there but not present, around but not available, at least not in the way they wanted them to be, with care and concern for them and their wellbeing. Thus the boys waited for parents like the ones they thought other boys had--the parents who would never come because they did not exist. They made up parents so the other boys would think the parents they were waiting for were good parents.

These boys also waited for the system to help. Hour upon hour, day upon day they waited for someone, something, to acknowledge them. They waited in line, for a placement with a good family, or for medical care. All this waiting drove them nuts. And still they waited, and simultaneously anticipated, as did I.

Like most youth, I anticipated driving my fathers car and having my own car, going up north, meeting a girl. I anticipated growing up, being free and on my own, the days when I could do what I wanted whenever I wanted, or so I thought. I would drive away, go up north at the drop of a hat, and have my own money to spend on the things I wanted. I anticipated seeing a friend again, a girl I loved, having a cat, getting a bike, swimming, becoming a professional basketball player.

Gradually, and more frequently the anticipation of the end of something took over from the beginning. For example, I would wait all year to go up north to spend time at a cabin on a warm inland lake with my family, then once I got there, I would worry about (anticipate) the end. As I got older, I became less and less excited about going, until I eventually would rather stay home with my friends. As a young man, I drank and used drugs to stay in a place where the anticipation of the beginning merged with the anticipation of the end. Ultimately, I would be let down because nothing lasted. It took me a while to get out of this and to learn to enjoy the moment, to just be without waiting or anticipating, a lesson of youth, learned through experience that shaped my happiness and fulfillment as an adult. Now I have a place up north I can go to almost any time I want and just be.

The youth I worked with, and try today to understand in hindsight, anticipated mostly bad things happening. Their dreams had been repeatedly unfulfilled. They had been disappointed time after time, got their hopes up only to be let down. Many of them began to anticipate these things happening, and did anything they could to avoid the future. For many of them there was no future. Friends had been killed, parents jailed, the world witnessed and experienced as a violent short-lived place. Others wanted no future or past. They wanted now, because that was, for the moment, the safest, least painful place. If they anticipated, something bad would surely happen, and often it did. Limbo was a better place.

SPACE AND PLACE

Like all youth, I often waited and anticipated in spaces and places where something might happen. I put myself where there was possibility. I was bored somewhere, positioned, "just in case" (Baizerman 1995). A girl I liked might show up or an older kid would drive by in a customized car and give me a ride. Usually these did not happen, but in these places it could. Or we might rumble or tumble in these places, the park or on the street corner.

They built a shopping mall on a field next to a creek that was our baseball diamond, and fishing place. A place of excitement replaced with something predictable, dependable, the same as other malls that followed. We found another place to do our thing. I sat on the shore of Lake Michigan and dreamt of being at sea, rode the train to the jazz festival in Chicago, which was like "another planet," and hitchhiked to New Orleans, a place unlike any other I had been.

What I am, is inseparable from these places. Often these are places where I am waiting near water as in my fragment poems. They shape me and the meaning I make of the world. I am the Midwest and New Mexico of my youth. The east side of Milwaukee, the duplexes and bungalows I grew up in and surrounded by. The horseback rides I took into the mountains.

My room is me. I shape this space and it shapes me (Maier, 1987, p 153-159). It is a predictable safe place, the room of my youth. It is also a boring place, a place of waiting, anticipating and longing to be somewhere else. Yet, I return, often, to "my room," or the room that *is* me. Like others, when I am away from home for too long, I seek familiar places. I enmesh myself in the waters of home, the familiar walls, and long for the familiar weather after a while. Memories are connected to these places and spaces as in the photos of my youth, leaning on an oar, sitting in my father's chair, looking like Ricky Nelson at the Thanksgiving dinner table.

I took two youth I worked with to thanksgiving dinner at Suzanne's parents' house. They did not know how to behave in this space and place. It was foreign, unfamiliar. Thanksgiving was not a place of happy memories for them. There hadn't been thanksgivings, at least not the way we remembered them, or if there was one, it was not happy. They were not fed at Thanksgiving. The trust that comes with being fed, in general, was not part of their experience. They acted out at Suzanne's parent's house. Threw the mashed potatoes. I had to discipline them. Eventually, they settled into the space, the home that was not their home, even though they might have wished it so. Meanwhile, Suzanne's parents got to see the work I did--the good and the bad of it, the joy and the sadness, the anger and excitement, the fulfillment, mixed in with the struggle.

Like many youth today, the youth I worked with, grew up in frightening places. The places in which they waited, the things that happened, usually were not good. The hood, the street corner, the alleys, were riddled with gangs, drugs, and crime. They "tagged" these places with graffiti to call them their own. They belonged in these places, and the places belonged to them for better or worse. Home was often a cold place without enough blankets and human warmth, a place of frigidness or gushing guilt ridden permissiveness, or both, or neither. Something in these places was better than nothing. Home was not a home, but a temporary dwelling or shelter, and sometimes not even that.

There were no trips up north, jazz festivals, or hitchhikes to New Orleans, as I had. If there were trips they were usually on the run from something rather than to something. They got away to other places to avoid being abused and often found themselves in places where they were abused again. The spaces and places shaped them and these were not the spaces and places of a happy youth, but rather spaces of horror, or of unpredictable and unrelenting disappointment. There was little sunshine in these places. Yet, they managed to find some. They turned their reservations of despair into the hood—a surreal world of crime, belonging, graffiti, drug deals, and shootings. These became their "real" worlds. What they did in these places and spaces was not acceptable, but it was understandable. These were places they hung out in, where something good might happen, even if it didn't. The war zones they wished were the playgrounds of a happier youth. They gazed at these worlds from the nonexistent backseats of their parents' cars, a cockeyed view, but their view.

LIGHT AND DARK

Light and dark and the interplay between the two are themes in my life, work and writing, as they were in these scenes from my youth, and my novel about youth work, *Floating.* As a youth, after having sex the first time, scared and excited, I swam far out into Lake Michigan thinking about how the bright stars above and the abyss below were connected to the movement of my body and arms. I created these states of light and dark as I swam away from something, the fear of closeness and intimacy, of loosing self in another person.

When I was a small boy, I dropped a replica of the Statue of Liberty I wanted badly into the Atlantic Ocean, to see how it felt. I told my mother I was glad my grandmother died so I could see how it felt and to make her feel bad, and to get a reaction. And I discovered that I had the power to influence and manufacture feelings, my own and others.

My conscious and unconscious actions and decisions, in this regard, delivered to me joy and sadness. The light and dark actions I take and the choices I make are part of my care for self or *ethos* (Foucault cited in Rabinow and Rose, 1994). I am neither light or dark, or good or bad, but both. The boy in the movie, *My Life as a Dog,* can't stop behaving badly, even though he knows it is making it more difficult for his dying mother. He is a good boy, but just when things are going well, he does something to change the situation, or he acts badly.

Many of the youth I worked with, and have observed, were like this. They did something bad just when everything seemed to be going well. They were "rascals," I used to say to myself, knowing something much deeper was going on for them. It was as if they could not trust good feelings and subsequently were compelled to do something to make sure they were not rejected, or left behind, or hurt again. I always got this. Not because my experiences were their experiences but because I had had this urge, as a child, to see and feel the other side of things. It provided protection and sense of control. On the one hand it was part of youth in general and on the other hand it was a defense for these youth against something very painful.

Once, I worked with a boy who crushed and ate part of a Coke bottle. Afterwards, he told me he did it because the physical pain he imposed on himself was a diversion from the deeper emotional pain he felt. It helped him get away from it all. For me, this was a troubling epiphany, for him, a way of life.

My sketches usually have this mix of light and dark, sometimes seen in the weather, other times in the words, and other times, in the attitudes. One rarely exists in a sketch without the other. The interplay between the two is essential to understanding human connections and attachments.

I cannot know one without the other, or stay in light or dark for very long. The weather always changes, day turns to night, and joy to sadness. So too it was with the boys, who never lingered for very long in one place, or if they did it was in the dark places created in their childhoods. They were afraid of the dark, more so than most children are afraid of the dark, and would do anything to avoid putting their heads on their pillows late at night when they were alone with their dark thoughts. And this was understandable, and is even more so now, when I think of it in the contexts of my sketches and interpretations.

*

These musings, from my sketching experiences and readings, will continue as they did in the past, spiraling forward and back through my mind, as I try to understand the meaning of these and other themes as they appear in my future sketches. This is, in my opinion, the essence of knowing and being *in* youth *with* youth. It is the substance, the source of question and discovery, that lets us do "real" youth work, our own, and with others.

Too much discussion today in our field and society, I believe, is on the outcome of youth. It is as if adolescence is a phase to get teenagers through into a good job. Youth today are often feared, rather than accepted as a being in a legitimate and significant period of life. We are goal and result focused with youth. They are youth only on their way to being productive adult citizens with good paying jobs. They are not youth, as we know it, or the youth that many adults seem to have forgotten.

We don't want them to linger in and experience youth to its fullest. We want them to get good grades and get on with it so they can compete in the global and local economies and buy things. Camps, community centers, group homes, and schools, are funded to get results, not to piddle around in the spaces and places of youth. Capitalism assesses them in relationship to the bottom line; youth has no use value (Krueger, 2005; Skott-Mhyre & Grretzinger, 2005). Youth are used for the sake of profit; a potential workforce, a means to an end, rather than an end (Magnuson, Baizerman, and Stringer, 2001). Their agency is not recognized.

The attitude is that they should stop the naval gazing and self-questioning. Figure it out, make decisions, get civically engaged, and get on with it. Choose your major, sooner rather than later, be fulfilled with a good job, nice family, and the trappings of the rich and middle class. If you have been abused and neglected, get over it and on with your life. Take responsibility for your actions, earn points for good behavior and forget about the past, you can't do anything about it anyways. So, you had a bad story, so did others, let go, move on and take charge of your own life. The imaginary audience and life are calling.

Yet fulfillment and productivity are not likely to be found unless they can fully experience their youth with caring adults. They have to be *in* it *with* others who care about them. We must understand this as we move, be still, wait, and anticipate with them in light and dark spaces and places that will change their stories and give them the hope that comes from being cared about in youth. We must bring our*selves* to our interactions and share the journey with them with presence, curiosity and understanding. Together we must also try to create moments of connection, discovery, and empowerment as is written about in the stories and literature of youth work (Fewster, 1990; Krueger, 2004; Maier, 1987, 1995). These moments in the spaces and places of hesitation motion, stillness, waiting, anticipating, light, dark, connection, discovery, and empowerment will change their stories for the better and when the time comes help them to be healthy adults.

"NO FARTING IN MY VAN"

When I got home, after presenting and discussing the thoughts above in Victoria, I thought about what I had learned and wrote my monthly column (Krueger, 2006, June) for www.cyc-net.org:

Late last month, I attended a child and youth care conference, Child and Youth Care in Action (love that title), at the University of Victoria. This was the first conference for graduates of their child and youth care program, community partners, and others interested in learning about some of the latest developments and approaches in the field. It was an excellent event and learning experience (as are all the conferences at the University of Victoria), with inaugural keynotes in the names of Henry Maier, and Gerry Beker, who I enjoyed seeing and talking with again. Like he did for many others in the field, Gerry helped me get my work published and has served as a mentor over the years. Henry Maier, as most of us know, died in 2004.

When I wasn't at the conference, I was with my friend Gerry Fewster. He has a beautiful home in Cowichan Bay, about 25 miles north of the city. We joked and "talked smart," as we usually do. We both see being in the moment and/or point of interaction as the key to child and youth care. If we can get this right, we believe everything else will follow, as we try to create moments of connection, discovery, and empowerment. You have to show up and be there first, in other words, before you can get anything to work.

Many of the workshops at the conference seemed to support this point of view. For example, I attended a workshop by Hans and Kathleen Skott-Mhyre, *Radical Youth Work: Love and Community,* in which they used post-Marxist concepts as a foundation for their discussion. During the workshop they said many intriguing things that got me thinking, none more than their use of Diego Rivera and Freida Kahlo as examples of revolutionaries—Diego, working from the outside to create change, and Freida from the inside out. And very interesting definitions of love and community that, these two career "direct line" workers offered, based on their experience and reading of philosophy and other literatures.

Previously, Doug Magnuson and I had written critical responses to Hans' challenging article in the *Child and Youth Care Forum*. As he and Kathleen spoke, I wished we had had a chance to speak and get to know each other beforehand. It was obvious that we shared many similar views. I really liked their definitions of love and community, and their emphasis on youth as agents of their own change.

When the discussion shifted to rules, they seemed to be saying much of what I had tried to say in my workshop titled, *Hesitation, Motion, Stillness, Space, Place, Light and Dark and other themes in Child and Youth Care*. Their feelings, like mine I think, were that in programs where people are self-aware and comfortable and confident in their personal authority few rules are needed because youth, even the most difficult ones, respond to these people with a sense of wanting to develop their own awareness and inner sense of boundaries. Youth respond, in other words, to the sincere, genuine, secure sense of the other self because this other self makes them feel safe, and open to exploring their own built in inner controls and feelings.

During the discussion one youth worker, a middle-aged man I had talked to earlier, after my workshop, a seemingly very experienced and competent street worker (I wish I remembered his name) said, "I don't care what you say, one rule I have is—" no farting in my van."

We all laughed, of course, but his point was well taken. In child and youth care, we need to know our own personal boundaries, as well as have some super-ordinate rules, not many, just a few to let the kids know that certain things simply are not permissible for anyone, like doing drugs or hurting others. Then, within this context of everyone pitching in around the big rules, situations can be handled as they arise in our interpersonal relationships.

Karen Vander Ven and others have written extensively about how point systems and handbooks of rules have gotten in the way of creative, and more fulfilling interaction in child and youth care. There does indeed seem to be a movement afoot to get back to personal relationships and developmental activities as the foundation for creating safe, invigorating, discovery filled, change oriented programs for children and youth. A central challenge in this movement I believe is finding the right balance of rules and personal authority and doing it according to the developmental needs of the child and youth care staff members who need time to develop the confidence, knowledge, skill, and intuition, which many of us more experienced workers developed over time. In the meantime, we have to continually work at being aware of our own boundaries and decide, which rules do we absolutely need to reinforce consistently? "No farting in my van," might be one that others find useful.*

*If the worker at the conference in Victoria reads this, please identify yourself and take credit for this delightful phrase. Your timing was perfect and an important part of my learning at the conference.

DEATH, WRITING, BULLS, AND WHITE NIGHTS

In this last chapter I present two more sketches *Death and Writing* and *Bulls and White Nights*, the first from my experimental autobiography and the second a new version of a favorite older sketch. This is part of the sketching process. I often try different combinations of sketches and fragments, each time learning something new or different about youth, self, and youth work. In addition to the themes I mused on in Chapter 7, loss, which is central to understanding life, youth, and youth work, is a theme in these sketches.

DEATH AND WRITING

(1987) The call comes at work.

"Your father is here. Something is wrong," Suzanne says.

I race to my house on Milwaukee's East Side. His car is parked on the front lawn. I enter through the enclosed porch. He's sitting glassy-eyed on the couch, with his hat to the side of his head.

"I'm doing badly, son." He used to say that when he was drunk, but he's not drunk now.

"I don't know how he got here in that condition," Suzanne says.

"Me either, son, I'm confused."

She puts his car on the street while I drive him to the hospital where they say he's had a stroke. They also discover cancer. There isn't much they can do. It's spreading. We celebrate his 80th birthday in the hospital. My brother, an airline executive, comes with his wife and a silver heart-shaped balloon.

Reluctantly, I take him home. His short-term memory is shot, but his long-term memory is better than ever. He tells me things he has not told me before. Like how his father was drunk when he fell off that roof and broke his neck.

"Which pills should I take now, son?"

"The ones with the red tape on the bottle, I just told you that a minute ago."

"Be patient, son."

His crusty toenails bother me. "Put your slippers on," I say one night while we're watching the Gray Fox, a story about an old time train robber who got out of prison and went on one more spree.

117

"Leave him alone," Devon says.

Later when I tuck my father in like a little boy, he asks, "Where's mother, son?"

"She's dead. She died five years ago, remember?"

"Yes, of course, it just slipped my mind. Be patient with me, son," he says again as I turn out the light and close the door.

(1997) I put Camus back on the shelf. The writing teacher wouldn't have liked him—too minimal. The innuendo would have driven her nuts--too many hidden meanings, not for me, but for her, the teacher who preferred authors who used lots of words, whereas, I liked a sense of parsimony.

She offered herself to me once, in a letter. I refused. There would be no more anticipation, and for sure no more laughter in the writing if I accepted, I was sure of it, as tempting as her offer might or might not have been.

Once, she pissed in a sink. We were at my cabin in the woods, and she was afraid to go out in the dark by her self. She told Suzanne and I the next day. We laughed. On another occasion she tapped drumsticks at the feet of a previous lover who was dancing with another woman. He got the point. I did something similar once, a Jose Greco routine. Not with a previous lover, but with two lovers I did not like. I tap danced around their bed, feet stomping like a Spanish dancer. I wanted to write like her too before I found my own voice, which came to me in anticipation of her response, as I sat across from her at the dining room table and read my work out loud to her. Tap, tap, tap.

(1954) "You want to see how to make a fast buck, I'll show you how to make a fast buck," my father says loudly in a sing/song voice to my mother after he gets home in the middle of the night. ...

"Conundrum, conundrum, conundrum," I repeat as I sit in his chair.

"Let's fuck some women," he shouts in the drunken stupor of his sleep.

(1987) He wants to go home. We hire an aide. Twice a week I take him to radiation treatment.

"Careful, I'm a real sissy," he says to the nurses. His body is covered with liver spots, and warts. I'm getting some myself.

"No, you're not," the nurses say to my father.

"If I can just get in one more summer of golf, son, then I'll be ready to join Mother," he says one day when I walk him to the house. When we get inside, he stops in front of the mirror in the foyer and smiles at himself, then, hunched over with pain, he puts his hands in his pockets and does a jig.

(1997) We met long before we got to know each other as teacher and student. I passed her, many times, as I ran on the bluffs where she walked. First, no gesture was made. Then we nodded, and then, "Hello," which is what she also said the first time I came to the door with my manuscript in hand.

"Hello, Runner."

"Hi Walker," I replied and looked at her. She had smooth, baby skin and prematurely gray hair. The handsome woman with the premature gray hair and baby skin, that's how I saw her, simple as that.

Her house, like her writing, was meticulous, everything just so: the paintings and color photocopies on the walls, the doily on the table between us, the ashtray beside the bed she tried to get me in, or I'd like to think she'd have liked to get me in.

She had a photo of me on the bulletin board in the kitchen. I saw it the night she drummed at the feet of her former lover, her new lover there in a Halloween costume, before it was consummated, I found out afterwards.

(1987) The second call comes at work also. The aide can't get in the house. The students in my adolescent development class at the university sense something is wrong, but don't know what. "Knowing loss is key to working with troubled youth," I often say in class, but only the one's who have experienced it get it.

I race across town. The aide is at the door. There is an indentation in his chair.

"You check down here, I'll check upstairs," I say to the aide and run up the stairs, past the picture of my mother in the flapper hat. His bed is made.

"Here he is!" the aide shouts.

I run down the stairs. He is on his back next to the sink where he must have been shaving, razor by his side, the water still running.

"Oh, blessed Jesus," she cries.

"Do you know CPR?" I ask.

She's shaking. I lean over him, seal my lips to his and blow a mouthful of the life he gave me into his limp body. There is some eerie gurgling. "No, don't come back," I say to myself, and blow again to no avail.

The paramedics arrive and drag his body, like a sack of waste, across the linoleum to the kitchen where there is more room to work. When they pull down his pants to check for a pulse, and jolt his body, I go into the living room and sit in his chair.

(1997) I leave the bookstore. I saw the writing teacher here, on the streets, last winter, not too long before she killed herself. She was doing better. The therapy and St. John's Wort were working, she said. I had my doubts. That was the last time I saw her. I learned about her death when I was out of town. Someone at work told me when I called in for messages. She had hanged herself in the basement: same way, same age, as her mother. "The cats are at my feet. I'm facing the big if," the last words she wrote in her diary.

It wasn't an ending she'd have approved of. "How amateurish to end by killing off your hero," she said that day when I brought over a draft of my last chapter of my novel about Daniel, "It was going so well until then."

I didn't go to the funeral. Funerals are bad literature. There is no sense of anticipation in testimonials written for the occasion, especially when death is the topic. So I stayed home and thought about her, as I am now, as I walk in the fog towards the bluffs where I used to see her, sentiment washing through me like the

119

moist air. "I must fight this off, the sentiment," I tell myself. It does no good to be sentimental, not even now when the writing teacher is dead.

"I want to write a novel about a troubled boy," I said that day I ran over with my draft of a novel about Daniel, and me.

"Come in and I will help you," she said.

A foghorn sounds in the distance. I continue walking toward the pavilion where she held workshops in summer. For a moment, I think I see her coming through the fog, but it's someone else, another woman.

"Hello," I say.

She smiles, unfettered by the sound of the word spoken out loud.

(1987) I remember again, the night I saw my father dancing in the moonlight.

"You can stop the procedure," a voice says over the walkie-talkie.

They wheel him out. "Let's pray together," the aide says.

"No thanks," I say, and sign the paper.

"You want me to stay?" she asks.

"No, I'll be fine."

They all leave. It feels good to be in the house alone. The warmth from his chair rises around me. Everything is still. I sit a long time, then go home, and in the months that follow finish my novel about Daniel.

BULLS AND WHITE NIGHTS

A young man on a horse approaches from the side of the hill in the forest, his silhouette intermittently reappearing between the trees. As the sound of the hoofs moves closer and closer, I lean on my cross country ski poles and watch. With his long coat flowing behind with the horse's tail, it's a majestic scene. I watch until he disappears over another hill, then I return to my cabin on a small lake and fall asleep near a warm heater:

About a year after we enroll him in modern dance, Daniel takes the stage wearing black running tights. Across his bare chest and arms are wisps of black, and red like in a Franz Klein painting. He jumps into the composer's aching harmonies: an ice skater gliding effortlessly, a Spanish dancer, feet stomping on the ground, chest out, arm circled overhead, a ballet dancer leaping. It's all there for those who care to see. He's trying to exorcise the demons from a horrifying childhood. At the end he's curled on the ground, an exhausted Nijinsky.

My stomach growls for something to eat. I put on my leather jacket and back between the tall white pines. At the stop sign, I turn up the heat then turn right. Ahead, two bulls are running in the ditch next to the road. I slow down, pull alongside and role down the window. The sound of their hoofs hitting the snow reminds me of the man on the horse I saw earlier. After the bulls turn into the woods, I continue over the open creek. The Moose Inn is down the road. Joe, the owner, added carpeting and female bartenders, but it is still a country bar by most appearances. The waitress steers me to a table beneath a beer sign where there is enough light to read.

"The usual?" she asks.

I nod, then I call my neighbor about the bulls, but no one answers. While I read and wait, an older couple at the bar tells a story about a cat that got caught in a chunk of snow behind the wheel of their pickup and was still alive when they got home. No one questions this. The Moose Burger arrives shortly. It's reliable like the story I'm reading, Brezin Lea, by Ivan Turgenev.

"I told the boys I had lost my way and sat down among them. They asked me where I was from and fell silent for a while in awe of me. We talked about this and that..." In Penguin Classics 1967 edition of Sketches from a Hunters Album, *p. 103.*

I sit and read a while longer, then say goodbye to the waitress and the bartender. On the way home my mind drifts out across a white cornfield towards the moon. Suddenly around a bend the two bulls appear in the middle of the road. The car swerves to the left and back across the road where it comes to rest in a ditch. With the red oil light flashing in the dash, the bulls stare at the car. For a moment I think I see the young man on the horse. He's wearing a Hessian hat and carrying a long spear, which he points at me then he smiles and disappears.

The bulls lumber across the road into the woods. Fortunately it only takes a moment to dig out. I keep my eyes riveted to the road the rest of the way home. The smoke coming from the chimney is a welcomed site. I stop to piss in the outhouse. It's cold, but I get it done, then stand on the hill over the lake a moment, listening to the wind make a sweet crying sound as it moves over the ice.

" ...in the darkness we saw a figure coming toward us......But we were mistaken, it was not he." (From Dostoyevsky's White Nights, the third night.)

I call my neighbor again about the bulls. He answers this time, thanks me, and says he will look for the "damn bulls." After warming myself by the fire, I work some more on my latest sketch about Daniel and the other boys I knew at the residential treatment center. I want to capture a moment of connection but can't get it right. A bat fooled out of hibernation by the heat, buzzes overhead, then crawls back into a small crack in the ceiling, all its energy spent with nothing to eat. Unable to write anymore, I put on my old military overcoat and take a walk on the frozen surface of the lake. It's quiet and still. In the faint light of day, I can hear my feet hit the ground like a distant heartbeat.

"...Like drizzle on embers,
Footsteps within me
Toward places that turn to air..."

From Octavio Paz A Draft of Shadows

... Near the water purification plant I enter a ravine that rises to the pavilion. Surrounded by the bluffs, it is a quiet, private, place. I rest a moment where the sun shines through the branches and listen to melting snow trickle towards the lake then run up the steps two at a time and look down into the cold water I once swam in on a warm summer night...

CLOSING COMMENT

In this book I have tried to show how I use sketching to make myself visible and learn from my experiences. I would like to think that this has helped me as a colleague Jerome Beker once wrote (1996) "hear it deep and look to the questions that do so much to determine the soul of our work." If this book has in some way helped the reader achieve a similar goal I shall be pleased.

I close with two fragment poems:

Wim Wenders (2001) on Images

"The continuity of movement
 must be true (p.163)
Images are more truthful
than stories
in the eyes
of a child

Montage and narrative
are like great sums (of images)

If image can't be taken
on its own terms
and at its own worth,

the sum of all that
would amount to nothing (pp. 326-327)"

Images of a Boy

The photo arrived
today with a note
that said   we haven't seen you

for a while

He looked tall and handsome
in the shadow
of Blue Lake

The deep purple
New Mexico sky
in the background

Later he came to me again
in a dream

naked in his infant search
for antiquity

I reached out for him
but he slithered away
in the blue neon light
of a dark night

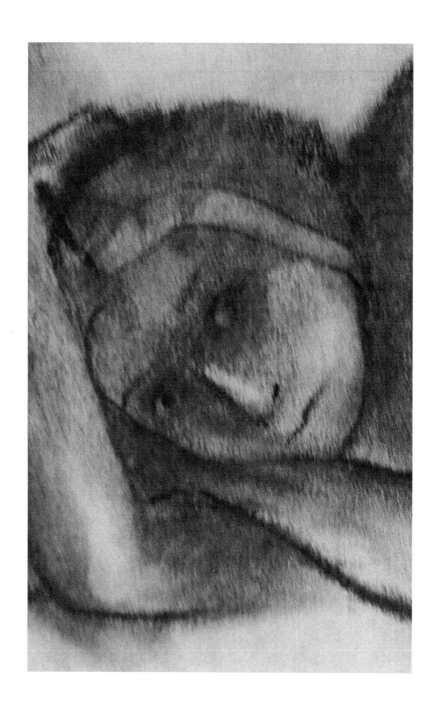

REFERENCES

Almereyda, M. (2003). *This so called disaster: Sam Shepard directs the late Henry Moss.* Documentary produced by Director Almereyda.

Anglin, J., Denholm, C., Ferguson. R. & Pence, A. (Eds.) (1990). *Perspectives in professional child and youth care.* New York: Haworth Press.

Austin, D. & Halpin, B. (1989). The caring response. *Journal of Child and Youth Care (Canada), 4,* 1-7.

Baizerman, M. (1992). Book review of Buckets: Sketches from the log book of a youth worker, by Mark Krueger. *Child and Youth Care Forum, 21,* 129-133.

Baizerman, M. (1995). Kids, place, and action(less). *Child and Youth Care Forum, 24,* 339-341.

Beker, J. (1996). Introduction: Calling our bluff. *Child and Youth Care Forum, 25,* 277-279.

Birkerts, S. (2006). Introduction. *Cream City Review, 30,* 1-10.

Bly, R. (Ed.) (1981). *Selected poems of Rainer Maria Rilke.* New York: Harper and Row.

Bruner, J. (1990). *Acts of meaning.* Cambridge, MA: Harvard University Press.

Brekhus, W., Galliher, J. & Gubrium, J. (2005). The need for thin description. *Qualitative Inquiry, 11*(6), 861-879.

Bruner, J. (1990). *Acts of meaning.* Cambridge, MA: Harvard University Press.

Carver, R. (1983). *Fires.* New York: Vintage Press.

Clough, P. (2002). *Narratives and fictions in educational research.* Philadelphia: Open University Press.

Csikszentmihalyi, M. (1990). *Flow: The psychology of optimal experience.* New York: Harper and Row.

Dejardins, S. & Freeman, A. (1991). Out of synch. *Journal of Child and Youth Care, 6,* 139-144.

Denzin, N. (2001). *Interpretive iInteractionism.* Thousand Oaks, CA: Sage Publications.

Denzin, N. & Lincoln, Y. Eds. (2004). *Handbook of qualitative research.* Thousand Oaks, CA: Sage Publications.

Denzin, N. & Lincoln, Y. Eds. (2000). Handbook of qualitative research. Thousand Oaks, CA: Sage Publications.

Deyhle, D. & Parker, L. (Eds.) (1999). *Race is—race isn't: Critical race theory and qualitative studies in education.* Boulder, CO: Westview Press.

Duras, M. (1986). *The lover.* New York: Harper and Row.

REFERENCES

Ellis, C. (2004). *The ethnographic I*. Walnut Creek, CA: Altamira Press.

Ellis, C. & Bochner, A. (2000). Autoethnography: Personal narrative. Reflexivity: Researcher as subject. In Norman Denzin and Yvonna Lincoln (Eds.) *Handbook of qualitative research*. Thousand Oaks, CA: Sage, 733-769.

Ellis, C. & Bochner, A. (1996). *Composing ethnography: Alternative forms of qualitative writing*. Walnut Creek, CA: AltaMira Press.

Fay, M. (1989). *Speak out*. Toronto: Pape Adolescent Center.

Fewster, G. (1999). Turning myself inside out: My theory of me. *Journal of Child and Youth Care. (Canada), 13*, 35-54.

Fewster, G. (1990). *Being in child care: A journey into self*. New York: Haworth.

Flyvbjerg, B. (2006). Five misunderstandings about case-study research. *Qualitative inquiry, 12*, 219-245.

Garfat, T. (1998). The effective child and youth care intervention. *Journal of Child and Youth Care, 12*, 1-178.

Halse, C. (2006). Writing/Reading a life: Rhetorical practice of autobiography. *Auto/Biography 14*, 95-115.

Humphreys, M. (2005). Getting personal: Reflexivity and autoethnographic vignettes. *Qualitative Inquiry, 11* (6), 840-860.

Jay, M. (2003). Critical race theory, multiculturalism, and the hidden curriculum of hegemony. *Mulitculturalism, 5*, 3-9.

Joyce, J. (1993). *Portrait of the artist as a young man*. New York: Penguin.

Kaufman, J. (2005). Autotheory: An autoenthograpic reading of Foucault. *Qualitative Inquiry, 11* (4), 576-587.

Kincheloe, J. (2005). On to the next level: Continuing the conceptualizing of the Bricolage. *Qualitative Inquiry, (11)* 3, 321-350.

Krueger, M. (2006). Pavilion: A portrait of a youth worker, three sketches. *Auto/Biography, (14) 1, 59-80*.

Krueger, M. (Ed.) (2004). *Themes and stories in youth work practice: In the rhythms of youth*. New York: Haworth Press.

Krueger, M. (2003). The quest to know: One man's inquiry into why he's home. Invited chapter for MaElwee, N. Jackson, A, Cameron, B. & Mckenna, S (Eds.) *Where have all the good men gone: Exploring males in social care in Ireland*. Athone IT, Ireland: Center for Child and Youth Care Learning.

Krueger, M. (2002). A further review of the development of the child and youth care profession in the United States. *Child and Youth Care Forum, 3*, 13-25.

Krueger, M. (1999). Presence as dance in work with youth. *Canadian Journal of Child and Youth Care, 13*, 59-72.

Krueger, M. (1995). *Nexus: A book about youth work.* Washington, DC: Child Welfare League of America.

Krueger, M. (1991a). A review and analysis of the development of professional child and youth care. *Child and Youth Care Forum, 20,* 379-388.

Krueger, M. (1991b). Coming from the center, being there, teaming up, meeting them where they're at, interacting together, counseling on the go, creating circles of care, discovering and using self, and caring for one another: central themes in professional child and youth care. *Canadian Journal of Child and Youth Care, 5,* 77-87.

Krueger, M. (1987). *Floating.* Washington, DC: Child Welfare League of America.

Krueger, M., Austin, M. & Hopkins K. (2004). Creating a culture that supports the development of staff. In Austin, M. & Hopkins, K. (Eds.) *Supervision as collaboration in the human services: Building a learning culture.* Thousand Oaks, CA: Sage.

Krueger, M., Evans, A., Korsmo, J. Stanley, J. & Wilder, Q. (2005). A youthwork inquiry. *Qualitative Inquiry 11* (3), 369-390.

Krueger, M. & Stuart, C. (1999). Context and competence in work with children and youth. *Child and Youth Care Forum. 28*(3), 195-204.

Lawrence-Lightfoot, S. (2005). Reflections on portraiture. *Qualitative Inquiry, 11,* (1) 3-15.

Markham, A.N. (2005). Go ugly early: Fragment narrative and bricolage as interpretive narrative. *Qualitative Inquiry 11* (6), 813-839).

Magnet, S. (2006). Protesting privilege. An autoethnographic look at whiteness. *Qualitative Inquiry, 21,* 736-749.

Magnuson, D., Baizerman, M. & Stringer, A. (2001). A moral praxis of child and youth care work. *Journal of Child and Youth Care Work, 15-16,* 302-313.

Maier, H. (1995). Genuine child and youth care practice across the North American continent. *Journal of Child and Youth Care (Canada), 10,* 11-22.

Maier, H. (1992). Rhythmicity – A powerful force for experiencing unity and personal connections. *Journal of Child and Youth Care Work, 8,* 7-13.

Maier, H. (1987). *Developmental group care of children and youth: Concepts and practice.* New York: Haworth.

Mattingly, M. (2002). North American certification project (NACP) competencies for professional child and youth care practitioners. *Journal of Child and Youth Care Work, 17,* 16-49.

McNaughton, C. (2006). Agency, structure, and biography: Charting transitions through homelessness in late modernity. *Auto/Biography, 14,* 134-152.

Nabokov, P. (1981). *Indian running.* Santa Fe, NM: Ancient City Press.

Nakkula, M. and Ravitch, S. (1998). *Matters of interpretation.* San Francisco: Jossey-Bass Publishers.

Oppen, G. (2003). *George Oppen selected poems.* New York: New Directions Books.

Ortiz, S. (1992). *Woven stone.* Tucson, AZ: University of Arizona Press.

REFERENCES

Rabinow, P. & Rose, N. (1994). *The essential Foucault.* New York: The New Press.

Rambo Ronai, C. (1998). Sketching with Derrida: An ethnography of a researcher/erotic dancer. *Qualitative Inquiry 4* (3), 404-420.

Redl, F. & Wineman, D. (1952). *Controls from within: Techniques for the treatment of the aggressive child.* New York: Free Press.

Richardson, L. (2000). Writing: A method of inquiry. In Denzin, K. & Lincoln, Y. (Eds.) *Handbook of qualitative research.* Thousand Oaks, CA: Sage, 923-948.

Richardson, L. (1994). Writing: A method of inquiry. In Denzin, K. & Lincoln, Y. (Eds.) *Handbook of qualitative research.* Thousand Oaks, CA: Sage, 516-529.

Rilke, J.M. (1984). *Letters to a young poet.* New York: The Modern Library.

Roth, P. (2001). *Shop talk.* Boston, MA: Vintage.

Roth, P. (1997). *American pastoral.* Newark, NJ: Vintage Press.

Sarris, G. (1993). *Keeping slug woman alive: A holistic approach to American Indian texts.* Berkeley, CA: University of California Press.

Skott-Mhyre, H. (2006). Radical youth work: Becoming visible. *Child and Youth Care Forum, 35,* 219-229.

Skott-Mhyre, H. & Grretzinger, M. (2005). Radical youth work: Creating a politic of mutual liberation for youth and adults: Part II. *Journal of Child and Youth Care Work, 20,* 110-127.

Strand, M. (2001a). *Hopper.* New York: Alfred A. Knopf.

Strand, M. (2001b). *The weather or words.* New York: Alfred A. Knopf.

Sparks, A. (2002). Fictional representations: On difference, choice, and risk. *Sociology of Sport 19,* 1-24.

Sudnow, D. (1979). *Talks body.* New York: Alfred A. Knopf.

Sudnow, D. (1978). *Ways of the hand.* New York: Alfred A. Knopf.

Tierney, W. (2000). Undaunted courage: Life history and the postmodern challenge. In Norman Denzin and Yvonna Lincoln (Eds.) *Handbook of qualitative research.* Thousand Oaks, CA: Sage, 537-555.

Vander Ven, K. (1999a). You are what you do and become what you've done: The role of activity in the development of self. Journal of Child and Youth Care (Canada), 13, 133-147.

Vander Ven, K. (1999b). Postmodern thought and its relevance to child and youth care work. *Child and Youth Care Forum, 28,* 294-301.

Ward, A. (2004). Toward a theory of the everyday: The ordinary and the special in daily living in residential care. *Child and youth care forum, 33* (3), 209-227.

Weaver, G. (1990). The crises in cross cultural child and youth care. In M. Krueger & N. Powell (Eds.) *Choices in caring.* Washington, DC: Child Welfare League of America.

Wenders, W. (2001). Wim Wenders: *On film*. London: Faber.

Wittgenstein, L. (2001). *Philosophical investigation*. Oxford UK: Blackwell Publishers Ltd.

ABOUT THE AUTHOR

Mark Krueger is a professor and director of the Youth Work Learning Center, University of Wisconsin-Milwaukee. Before coming to the university, he was a youth worker, and before that a youth in Milwaukee. He has written eleven books, including two novels, and dozens of research articles, and stories. For many years he has also been an active participant in the international effort to improve the quality of care for youth. Much more about him is shown in the pages of this book.

LaVergne, TN USA
07 October 2009
160133LV00001B/86/A